The first 100 years of

HAMPDEN

The Official Centenary Book

A story in words and pictures

By FORREST ROBERTSON and DAVID ROSS

4

Published by First Press Publishing,
One Central Quay, Glasgow, G3 8DA

Edited and designed by First Press Publishing.

ISBN - 1 901603 180

Printed and bound in Scotland

A HUNDRED years of drama, triumph, tragedy and heart-stopping excitement… Hampden has seen it all.

Unforgettable games, historic events, superstars of sport and music, riots and infernos – Scotland's colossal National Stadium has a story like no other.

It has played host to Matthews and Maradona, Johnstone and Jagger, Pele and Puskas, the Tartan Army and Tina Turner.

The world's greatest game. The world's greatest player scoring the world's greatest goal.

Where else could all of this take place than in the world's greatest stadium – Hampden Park, in Glasgow.

This story of Hampden Park contains many stunning and evocative photographs – certain to bring back many memories of a great stadium and great occasions.

That's what this book is all about.

The Publishers would like to thank the following for
their assistance in the production of this book:

Queen's Park Football Club

The Scottish Football Museum

BT Scotland
(sponsors of the BT Scotland South Stand and the
Official Centenary Book)

The Scottish Daily Record & Sunday Mail Ltd
(for access to their picture library)

Peter Colvin
(for the speedway photograph in Chapter 6)

Keith McAllister
(for the photograph of Hampden in 1905 – Page 26)

Jack Murray
(for the postcard of Hampden's first game – Page 28)

TREASURES ON SHOW: The Scottish
Football Museum at Hampden.

ZZ'S TOPPER: A picture of concentration and timing, Zinedine Zidane swings his foot and unleashes the wonder volley that crashed past the Bayer Leverkusen keeper, above and right, to secure the Champions League trophy for Real Madrid in the memorable 2002 final at Hampden – an event commemorated by the official "Glasgow Final 2002" programme, top right.

Wonder Goal at the Field of Dreams

THE ball swung lazily out of the floodlit night. Waiting at its estimated point of re-entry, the striker watched its flight intently, shuffling a few hesitant steps to shrug off his marker but totally focused on the imminent arrival from his left. Now, the textbook answer to this situation would have been to cushion the ball on chest or thigh, bring it down and shoot – but the man of the moment was Zinedine Zidane… and he doesn't care for textbooks.

The ball was a little over hip height when Zizou twisted his body and flailed the night air with his left – supposedly "wrong" – leg, connecting on the volley to send the ball flashing past the goalkeeper and high into the net. For a second or two there was a stunned silence, then uproar as 50,000 voices bellowed their admiration of one of Hampden's most spectacular moments, a goal that, almost incidentally, won the 2002 UEFA Champions League Final for Zidane and Real Madrid. Their 2-1 victory over Bayer Leverkusen meant a record ninth European crown for the La Liga giants – 42 years after another glory night against German opposition on the same ground. It was the spectacular highlight of a memorable occasion. That the world's greatest player should score one of the game's greatest goals for the world's greatest club at the world's greatest and oldest international football stadium was pure theatre.

Hampden Park, on Glasgow's South Side, had been so transformed in the 1990s that the Union of European Football Associations had awarded it a five-star rating, representing facilities of the highest standard, on and off the pitch. UEFA demands access to the ground and its amenities for supporters, teams and dignitaries that meet strict criteria. At Hampden, the car parking is ample, with a secured section for guests. Team coaches and VIP cars arrive at an underground entrance and are steps away from the players' dressing room or elevators that whisk the great and the good to eyrie-like lounges and seating below the rafters.

There is modern, comfortable seating for 52,063 paying customers. Reception areas for supporters, players and

SOARING SUCCESS: Millions of football fans throughout the world were thrilled by the way Hampden staged the UEFA Champions League Final in 2002. The spectacular pre-match entertainment was equalled by the quality of the game itself.

officials are of the highest standard, as are catering facilities for all.

The quality of the dressing rooms for players, referees, linesmen and even ballboys and girls exceeds those in the poshest country clubs and their every need is considered and catered for. There are 22 lockers in both the home and away dressing rooms because UEFA require space for 11 players plus nine stripped substitutes. There are separate lockers and shower facilities for team coaches and back-up staff.

There is space for four match officials in both referees' changing rooms – "both" because there are separate facilities for males and females.

Hampden has met UEFA's demand that the "warm-up" area is surfaced in the very latest in artificial grass technology and positioned between the dressing rooms and the pitch.

The facilities of the National Stadium Sports Medicine Centre, the permanent medical facility situated deep within the main building, are second to none. Members of the press, TV and radio have comfortable seats in which to relax and have access to every electronic resource they could require.

And then there is the pitch. The 105 metre by 68.5 metre playing surface is further surrounded by at least five metres of grass. Its camber is just right, the surface true and the quality perfect.

Indoors, Hampden boasts the Scottish Football Museum – the first facility of its kind in the world – convention facilities, exhibition halls, office suites and catering amenities.

The Scottish Football Association, the Scottish Football League, Scottish Premier League, Queen's Park Football Club and the Affiliated Associations have all located their headquarters at Hampden, which can only encourage closer co-operation.

And yet Hampden Park in the 21st century is more than just a big football ground. The arena is one of the country's leading events centres where rock stars such as the Rolling Stones, Rod Stewart, Eminem, Bon Jovi and Robbie Williams have performed.

World boxing titles have been won and lost, rugby and hockey internationals staged. International speedway, athletics, tennis exhibitions, American football, baseball exhibitions, youth organisation assemblies, royal visits, religious meetings, helicopter displays and movie star visits – all have graced the Hampden scene.

Many stars have dazzled at this world-famous arena but Hampden is a superstar in its own right. And what a story it has to tell.

15

LET IT ROCK: Rod Stewart in
action at Hampden in 1999,
opposite page, while American
rockers Bon Jovi pack them in,
above.

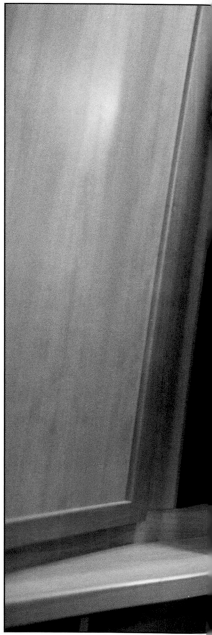

ONLY THE BEST: The revamped Hampden was designed with players and fans in mind. Facilities such as the hydrotherapy pool, far left, and the dressing-rooms are the last word in luxury and practicality and are the envy of football authorities throughout the world.

FIELD OF DREAMS: Joy and despair, cheers and tears... Hampden has seen them all over the past hundred years.

PIONEERS: The Queen's Park team in their famous black and white hoops pose with a side from Copenhagen in 1900.

Chapter 1

The English Patriot and a Scottish Institution

THE current site of Scotland's National Stadium was, until late on in the reign of Queen Victoria, a piece of spare grassland split by a burn and surrounded by farms. Its transformation into one of the wonders of the early 20th century was due almost entirely to the foresight and determination of a quite unique sporting institution, Queen's Park Football Club.

Its founders were a group of Highland "gentlemen" who lived and worked and played in Glasgow in the mid-1860s. On summer evenings they would arrange to meet at the Queen's Park recreation grounds on the south side of the city. There, they would drop their jackets for goals, produce their leather football and set about their favourite game with vigour and skill. In July 1867, they formed their own club named after their ground – The Queen's Park Football Club. A year later, their secretary wrote to The Thistle club from Glasgow Green to invite them to turn out at the recreation grounds on August 1, 1868. The letter added: "Be good enough to bring your ball with you in case of any breakdown". The letter can be seen today in the Scottish Football Museum at Hampden. It is the oldest surviving correspondence relating to a football fixture anywhere in the world.

Queen's met and defeated clubs from Airdrie, Hamilton and Glasgow over the next three years as well as playing scratch games among themselves and others, but the spur to greater things came when the Football Association's Charles Alcock wrote to the Glasgow Herald in November 1872 to ask for native Scottish players to compete against an English select in an official international match. The challenge game took place at the West of Scotland Cricket and Football Club's ground at Hamilton Crescent, Partick, on St Andrew's Day, November 30, 1872.

Queen's represented Scotland in their then club colours of navy blue jerseys, white athletic knickers and red socks and comfortably held the white-dressed southerners to a goal-less 90 minutes. A crowd of 4,000 had crammed into the ground, with dozens more perched on trees and on the roofs of cabs, to watch the exhibition of skill and excitement.

The success of the match made Queen's Park realise they required a private ground of their own. They asked the Glasgow Corporation Parks Department for land on the east side of Langside Road but were refused. It wasn't until October 1873 that the council was persuaded to lease them a stretch of land on the east side of Cathcart Road in the shadow of Prospecthill. Five days later, the Queen's pulled on their new black-and-white hooped jerseys to meet and beat Dumbreck FC in their very first Scottish Cup tie.

What about a name for the new ground? A few years earlier, housebuilders George and Alexander Eadie had erected rows of tenements on Prospecthill. The most prominent was named after John Hampden, a 17th-century English Parliamentarian who had fought in the Civil War. And so a long-forgotten English patriot achieved immortality through Scottish football.

The first Hampden Park lasted 10 years until the Cathcart and District Railway Company announced plans for a new line which cut through the west terrace. It forced the club to move 150 metres north-east to land leased from Dixons, the iron manufacturers.

This second Hampden Park opened in October 1884 and had ample room for expansion. It was developed to a level never seen before and soon the facilities extended to a two-storey, brick-built pavilion including changing rooms, baths, committee rooms, a gymnasium and recreational space and a ground capacity in excess of 25,000.

But when Queen's Park requested more land for development, they received an emphatic refusal from their landlords.

The hunt for a third Hampden had begun.

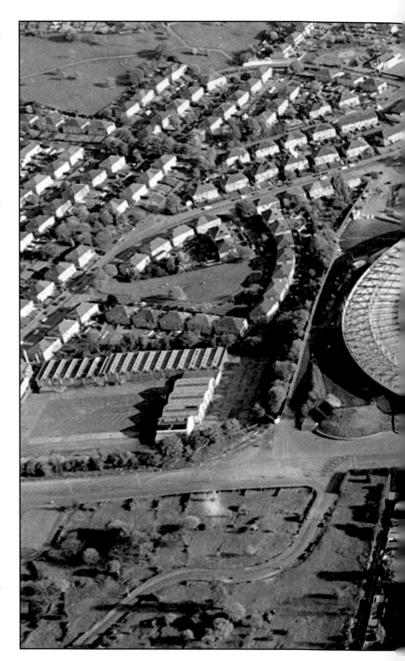

POPULAR GROUND: The Hampden terraces are already packed but many more fans are still queueing outside for this game in 1905.

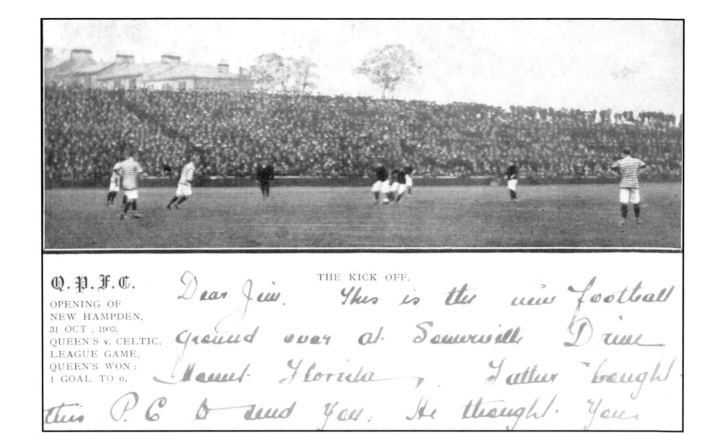

Q. P. F. C.

THE KICK OFF.

OPENING OF
NEW HAMPDEN,
31 OCT., 1903.
QUEEN'S v. CELTIC.
LEAGUE GAME,
QUEEN'S WON:
1 GOAL TO 0.

Dear Jim. This is the new football ground over at Somerville Drive Mount Florida. Father bought this P.C. to send you. He thought you

PIONEERS: When it was opened on October 31, 1903, Hampden was the biggest and best football ground in the world. This postcard, above, marks the opening game between Queen's Park, in their famous black and white hoops, and Celtic.

Chapter 2

The Biggest Football Ground in the World

IN the 30 years leading up to the end of the 19th century, rural Langside and Mount Florida effectively ceased to exist. The farms, milking sheds, byres and orchards disappeared under villas, rows of tenements, churches, schools and all manner of industry. Queen's Park's options seemed also on the way out… until Henry Erskine Gordon came to the rescue.

Erskine owned extensive land in the district and agreed to sell the footballers a portion on the south side of Prospecthill, where he had allowed Mount Florida Cricket Club to bat and bowl. Queen's would get about 12 acres in front of the newly-built Somerville Drive tenements for the sum of £10,000 on condition that the club paid half of the sewer and street costs and, importantly, the diversion of the Mall's Myre Burn into a brick culvert. The burn ran across the field but its existence explains the excellent drainage the ground has enjoyed for more than a century. With satisfactory arrangements made with agricultural tenants at Clincart Farm, the deal was done in November 1899.

The ground took shape slowly over the following three and a half years. The pitch was shifted northwards so the slope from Somerville Drive could be incorporated into the terracing. The proposed concrete cycle banking around the pitch was scrapped to increase the terracing capacity by 17,000 and James Miller – who had won a small architectural competition – oversaw the construction of his designs for twin stands, both with a capacity of 2,200, while capacity rose to an overall 40,000. The design and construction of the terracing was carefully considered following disaster at Ibrox Park in 1902. During a Scotland v England match a portion of the wooden west terrace at Ibrox had collapsed, leaving 25 spectators dead and more than 500 injured.

Hampden's terraces were firmly set on earth banks and made use of innovative penning and barrier arrangements. The proposed pavilion between the two stands was put on hold for cost reasons.

For several years, the club rented a ground-floor flat at 113 Somerville Drive as a temporary headquarters. Nevertheless, on October 31, 1903, the new stadium sat ready and waiting.

The crowds that streamed out to Mount Florida that afternoon for the grand opening of "New Hampden Park" gazed on a vastly different scene to the one we are familiar with today. Clincart Farm nestled to the immediate west and the rolling farmland of what is now King's Park, Castlemilk and Hangingshaw stretched off to the south and east. The stands were somewhat gap-toothed in appearance and the open terraces on the three other sides, although quite incredible to a 1903 audience, would appear quite shallow to a modern fan.

Glasgow's Lord Provost Sir John Ure Primrose performed the opening ceremony, accompanied by representatives of the SFA, the English FA, the Scottish League, Rangers, Celtic, Partick Thistle, Third Lanark and a host of other dignitaries and former top players. After a hearty cheer and the unfurling of the Queen's Park flag, Sir John declared the ground open.

Celtic were the opponents in a league game and the Spiders, perhaps sensing destiny deserved a supreme effort, punched above their weight and won 1-0. From a cross by J.L. Logan in the second half, David Wilson sent the ball skidding past Celtic keeper Davy Adams – Hampden's first ever goal.

The mammoth new arena – the biggest in the world at the time – had no trouble attracting cup finals and internationals and developed quickly into the natural home of the country's national game. The first "big game", the 1904 Scottish Cup Final, pitted Celtic against Rangers. They served up a cracker.

A temporary pavilion had appeared between the main stands, looking like a little medieval jousting stand, and the terraces had been increased, so the 64,472 who paid over their sixpences and shillings that afternoon created

CROWD CONTROL: The terraces at Hampden were firmly set

on earth banks and made use of innovative barrier and penning arrangements – as illustrated in this picture from the late 1950s.

SCRUM GAME: The Scotland and South Africa players before the rugby international at New Hampden Park in 1906. It was almost a hundred years before the nation's rugby men returned to the ground.

a new Scottish record. Celtic won 3-2 thanks to a hat-trick by Croy miner Jimmy Quinn – the first in a cup final. Tom Robertson, who refereed the game, is to date the only man to play in a winning cup team, officiate at a final and be president of the SFA.

England's bow before the famous slopes in April 1906 created enormous interest. The crowd started to converge on Mount Florida four hours before kick-off, arriving in hundreds of special trains, tramcars, by new-fangled motor cars, horse carriages and on foot. By 3pm, 102,741 people – an attendance never seen before in Scotland – jammed into the ground and the home side responded by coasting through the match. Jimmy Howie scored twice to give the Scots a 2-1 victory.

Hampden was now unopposed for the international against the Auld Enemy and never again did the English cross the border without making it their destination. However, it wasn't just the football authorities who had been impressed by the majestic new stadium. The Scottish Rugby Union rented Hampden on November 17, 1906, to host the visit of the South Africans, who had made sensational progress around the British Isles, winning all their games. The SRU realised that no rugby ground was capable of satisfying the public's hunger to see these megastars. They were well rewarded with an attendance of more than 30,000 and a stirring 6-0 home win on the back of K.G. McLeod's two tries. International rugby did not reappear in Glasgow for 90 years.

A new world record crowd of 121,452 was in place in 1908 for a Scotland v England clash that ended in a 1-1 draw. In 1910, more than 60,000 began singing their hearts out on the terraces almost three hours before kick off and a further 45,000 "latecomers" crammed in to witness an easy 2-0 win for Scotland.

Hampden was the cup final venue in 1905 when Third Lanark triumphed over Rangers after a replay and the stadium hosted the action again in 1907 and 1908 as Celtic brushed aside Hearts 3-0 then St Mirren 5-1.

Hampden was again the stage in 1909 as Celtic tried to defend their crown against Rangers. There were two attempts to find a winner, with the matches attracting a total of 131,000 people. But rioting at the end of the replay resulted in the trophy being withheld for the only time in its history. It had started innocently enough. Jimmy Quinn opened the scoring for Celtic in the April 10 final but Gilchrist and Bennett scored in the space of five minutes to put Rangers in command.

Late on, Hoops winger Dan Munro swung over a ball, more in hope than expectation. Rangers keeper Harry Rennie caught it under his bar before stepping aside to evade the in-rushing Quinn. But referee J.B. Stark, of Airdrie, sparked fury when he ruled the keeper had crossed his line with the ball – a decision Rennie disputed to his dying day.

In the replay, Jimmy Gordon opened for Rangers after 20 minutes and Celtic equalised in the second half when Quinn hit his sixth cup final goal. But confusion over whether the match should go to a replay brought disastrous consequences when referee Stark blew for time up.

Puzzled players from both sides milled at the centre circle, unsure what to do, while fans – who believed the game would be played to a conclusion – demanded that extra time be played.

The clamour grew until there were thousands of disgruntled fans on the grass. Police tried pushing protesters back to the terraces but trouble erupted and a full-scale battle began.

Goalposts were uprooted and a gang paraded a crossbar up the east terrace. Corner flags were used as weapons, coshes and pokers appeared, bottles, bricks and stones flew, payboxes were smashed and set on fire and when the fire brigade arrived, they

THE RIOT ACT: Flames and smoke belch into the air as Old Firm fans go on the rampage against the authorities after the 1909 Scottish Cup Final at Hampden Park, right. The disgraceful scenes were repeated during the 1980 Final when police used horses to clear hooligans off the pitch, next page.

were attacked, their hoses cut and the pieces thrown on to the fire to keep it ablaze. Yards of torn-up fencing were also set alight using oil stolen from a nearby garage.

At the height of the two-hour riot, it is estimated that 5,000 fans were involved. Ambulancemen tending the injured were attacked with boot and fist.

With reinforcements dashing to the ground from all parts of the city, the police eventually forced the mob out into the streets, where they marched back to town brandishing their weapons and smashing windows.

Horrified officials from Queen's Park, the Old Firm clubs, the SFA and the police surveyed the wrecked ground on Sunday morning and instantly agreed that a further replay was out of the question. The cup was withheld.

That there was a cup to play for in the future was thanks to the quick-wittedness of Tom Maley, brother of the Celtic manager Willie, who grabbed the silver trophy along with the gate receipts of £1,400 and took refuge with them in a nearby house.

Bigotry was not the cause of the riot – suspicion of financial exploitation was. There had been several mysterious draws in various national and local cup competitions between the Glasgow pair over the preceding few years and the press had been quick to point this out to the paying public in print and cartoon, most famously in the Scottish Referee of April 16, 1904, which featured a man whose sandwich board urged the masses to "PATRONISE THE OLD FIRM – RANGERS CELTIC Ltd" – a cartoon that was the origin of the famous nickname.

The SFA shied away from Hampden and

the final did not return until after the 1914-18 war. Ibrox and Parkhead hosted pre-war finals to subdued crowds of no more than 60,000.

The Hampden Riot pushed Queen's Park into making major ground improvements. The wooden payboxes with their tin roofs gave way to the brick-built ones at the Somerville Drive corner with their castle battlements frontage which was familiar to arriving fans for more than 80 years. There was more than a hint that their fort-like appearance was a deliberate attempt to dissuade visitors from repeating the 1909 lawlessness. A substantial brick wall went up around the ground to replace the timber fencing and additional banking of the terraces pushed capacity up to 125,000 by 1910. The little wooden pavilion settled snugly between the stands had always been a temporary measure but a new one did not arrive until 1914.

Almost 11 years after the ground's inauguration, a new brick-and-steel centre stand went up. It seamlessly blended in with the west and east structures and had a traditional Scottish crow-stepped gable front in brick-and-white roughcast.

The stand provided a large reading room, committee rooms, gym, club offices, changing rooms with showers

THE FORTRESS: The turrets gave Hampden a fort-like appearance. Perhaps a reminder to unruly fans to behave themselves. This picture was taken in the late 1940s.

and baths on the ground floor. Along a passageway, down a flight of stairs and along another corridor was the referee's room. Hospitality suites were on the first floor and upwards still in the crow's nest was a Press Box with seats and unimpeded views for 102 newspapermen. No mobile phones in those days, no laptops with internet connection – these newshounds shared just six external phone lines, plus telegraphic services brought in after considerable debate for £44. The Queen's Park club showed their eye for a business deal when they sold the old pavilion to Dundee. Hampden now sat in stately splendour, all debt paid off.

The ground capacity stretched like elastic for the 1912 Auld Enemy clash. A new world record attendance of 127,307 looked on as Andy Wilson scored after just seven minutes with a speculative shot that English keeper Bob Williamson fumbled over the line before Holley slammed home an equaliser from close range.

The gate was down to 105,000 for the 1914 International and Scotland dominated thanks to superior teamwork. Charlie Thomson was their star, marshalling his defence from the centre-half position and setting up the playmakers in his inimitable style. He caused a sensation by volleying home from 25 yards after a first-minute corner. It is doubtful if Sam Hardy in the English goal even saw the ball. England equalised before the interval

RUNNING GAME: Ever since the early years Hampden has hosted important athletics meetings. Here J.S. Smith, of Canon ASC, wins the 10 mile race in the Glasgow Championships, held at the stadium in April 1933.

but Jimmy McMenemy put the Scots ahead again and Willie Reid's tap-in gave the home side a 3-1 victory.

The Scottish Amateur Athletics Association had long seen Queen's Park as a good friend and host of its annual championships. In these early years, the SAAA held its cross-country championships at the new Hampden which, with its rural setting, was an ideal setting-off point for the runners, who reappeared after a bracing dash around the local fields and farms.

Scotland's athletes competed against Ireland and England in triangular internationals at Mount Florida in 1914 – an event that returned in 1922, 1926 and 1930.

Football continued during the First World War, both as a diversion and as a ripe venue for recruiting to the armed forces. However, the SFA suspended its national cup competition and abandoned internationals for the duration.

Hampden, although far from deserted during the war, subsisted on a phoney, drab diet of league games and charity matches at various levels, including the final of the 1918 Army and Navy War Fund Shield, a mini League Cup competition involving Celtic, Clydebank, Kilmarnock, Morton, Motherwell, Queen's Park, Rangers and Third Lanark.

Celtic beat Morton in the final.

IMPOSING: The front of Hampden in the 1960s. The crow-stepped gable can be seen quite clearly.

EXPANSION: In the early 1920s the stadium was extended and a new Lesser Hampden was constructed.

Chapter 3

Hampden Goes Roaring Through the Twenties

HAMPDEN was chosen as the venue for a Victory International against England in May 1919 to mark the end of the First World War. Although the attendance was a relatively disappointing 80,000, and the result was an even more disappointing 4-3 defeat for the hosts, normal service had been resumed. Yet still the stadium's owners were not satisfied with their arena, and continued to strive for perfection. Over the next few years, the ground surrounding the stadium was purchased, new roads were laid and a new Lesser Hampden constructed. By the end of the 1920s, the King's Park terracing was extended to accommodate a further 25,000 spectators and Hampden itself spread over 33 acres.

Apart from the unofficial Victory match, it had been seven long years since international football had been staged at Hampden, so the anticipation surrounding the fixture against England in April 1921 was intense. Adding spice to the occasion, Scotland had a chance to secure the International Championship outright for the first time since 1910 and with maximum points for the first time in the 20th century.

All they had to do was win but they had an inexperienced side. None of the Scotland XI were pre-war internationals, there were three players making their debuts and the Scots' most experienced star didn't even play in either the Scottish or English Leagues – Central League Dunfermline's Andy Wilson, making his sixth appearance for his country.

There were fears that a transport strike and increased admission charges would reduce the gate but while down on pre-war figures, there were still around 85,000 in the ground to see Wilson give Scotland the lead after 20 minutes. Rangers' left wing pairing of Andy Cunningham and Alan Morton controlled the game and "Wee Blue Devil" Morton scored his side's second with a long-range effort before Cunningham sealed a 3-0 victory with a

WHAT A TO DO-O! There were amazing scenes at Hampden after Kilmarnock, pictured above, won the Scottish Cup for the first time in 1920. A flock of pigeons was released after the game to carry the great news back to Ayrshire.

header after 57 minutes. The Auld Enemy soundly thrashed and the championship secured with maximum points, there couldn't have been a more triumphant return to the international arena for Scotland's premier football stadium.

Cup football had returned to Hampden in a low-key fashion in the spring of 1919 with a Junior Cup semi-final won by St Anthony's. They went on to lose to local side Rutherglen Glencairn in a replayed final in front of 38,000. The 1920 and 1921 Junior Finals also went to Hampden but it hosted only three more before World War Two. The ground's full-time association with the Juniors came later.

When the Scottish Cup resumed in 1919-20, few would have predicted the identity of the two finalists. Neither Kilmarnock, with one solitary losing appearance in the Scottish game's biggest club match, nor Albion Rovers – who were then bottom of the league – would have been expected to adorn the showpiece occasion.

The SFA assumed a low turn-out on April 17, 1920, and thought it was safe to return the final to Hampden – they got it 50 per cent right. Such was the post-war appetite for football that an amazing 95,000 poured through the turnstiles, creating a new Scottish Cup Final record. Thousands more were left disappointed when they were locked out as the game kicked off. Those who managed to get in were treated to a richly entertaining game as underdogs Rovers grabbed a fifth-minute lead.

Killie came back to equalise before the interval, then took the lead two minutes after the restart. The Coatbridge outfit weren't finished, though, and levelled almost immediately. With half an hour remaining, JR Smith fired what proved the winner for Killie and their fans greeted the club's first cup triumph with a thunderous roar and the release of a flock of pigeons to carry the news back to Ayrshire.

Smith earned a place in football history three years later when he scored for Bolton in the first Wembley FA Cup Final, becoming the first player to score in finals at both historic venues.

Rangers' unlikely opponents in the 1922 Scottish Cup Final were unfancied Morton. But in a match described by one club official as "the roughest final I've seen in 40 years", the Greenock side stunned themselves and their fans in the 75,000 crowd by winning 1-0 thanks to Jimmy Gourlay's goal from a free-kick after 11 minutes. Delirious Morton officials remembered then they hadn't presumed to bring champagne with them, so manager Robert Cochran hastily ran off to "borrow" some from Queen's Park. Hampden Park on April 15, 1922, remains Morton's finest hour.

Bathgate's visit to Hampden for their Scottish Cup second-round tie against Queen's Park on January 17, 1923, may not have sounded glamorous but it attracted more than 50,000 – many of them hoping to catch a glimpse of the stadium's first royal visitor. The Duke of York – the future King George VI – popped in during a two-day visit to Edinburgh and Glasgow. What His Royal Highness thought of a dull 1-1 draw is not recorded but he did leave the ground 10 minutes before the end.

Neither Queen's nor Bathgate were inspired by regal support to make it all the way to the final that year, leaving the stage free for Celtic and Hibernian. The famous slopes were swathed in

RUB OF THE GREEN: Celtic's Patsy Gallagher evades the Hibernian defence in the 1923 Scottish Cup Final, above.

....

DOUBLE TOPPER: Airdrie's Hughie Gallagher scored twice in Scotland's 2-0 defeat of Auld Enemies England in 1925, left.

green favours as Celtic's Joe Cassidy headed the goal that delighted most of the 80,000 present and brought the trophy back to Parkhead.

For the 1923 international against England, the SFA decided to stick to a minimum admission price of two shillings (10p), which was considered steep at the time. It reduced the crowd to 71,000. England drew first blood when Burnley's Bob Kelly headed home. Rangers' Andy Cunningham levelled but Vic Watson of West Ham put the English in front again three minutes from half-time. On 55 minutes it was Andy Wilson, playing in his final international, who pounced to level the score at 2-2. Scotland failed to snatch a winner but, for once, it didn't matter. They had won the international crown for the third year in a row – an achievement beyond any other Scotland side either before or since. Their triumph belonged to one of the early 20th century's great players. This was Wilson's 13th goal in 12 full internationals. a superb record for any era but particularly so in the days when the offside law demanded the presence of three opposing players between the attacker and the goal.

The SFA had shared the cup final between Ibrox and Parkhead following the 1909 riot but, after Airdrie defeated Hibs in the 1924 final at Ibrox, Hampden returned to favour and finally reigned supreme over Celtic Park and Ibrox thanks to an unlikely source – the regional manager of the London, Midland and Scottish Railways. The Cathcart Circle to Mount Florida and Kings Park was the only line in Glasgow which could cope with the massive increase in traffic when a big game was on. Railway staff were placed at quarter-mile intervals by the track and hand-flagged the specials through to Hampden.

It has remained the home of the cup final ever since, with the exception of a few years at the end of the 20th century when the Grand Old Lady was getting a facelift.

★ ★ ★ ★ ★

WITH the big football games bypassing Hampden in 1924, athletics took centre stage. The Olympics were due in Paris that summer so the Scottish AAA Championship at Hampden in June took on special significance. Eric Liddell limbered up by winning the 110 yards, 220 yards and 440 yards races at Mount Florida. He then triumphed in Paris in the 400 metres before famously refusing to compete in other events on a Sunday due to his religious convictions.

Liddell's athletics swansong in Britain was at Hampden in 1925. After that he travelled across Siberia by train to China, where he taught as a missionary for many years before dying in 1945 in a Japanese internment camp. His exploits were immortalised in the film Chariots Of Fire.

Queen's Park had a long association with amateur athletics. Their outside right Jimmy Crawford – the last amateur to play in a full international against England – won a sprint title at Hampden in the late 1920s.

The SAAA Championships continued almost exclusively at Hampden throughout the 1920s and

FLYING SCOTSMAN: Eric Liddell wins the 220 yard sprint final for a record fifth time at the Scottish AAA Championships at Hampden in 1925.

RECORD GATES: Six-figure crowds were regular occurrences at Hampden in the 1920s. In this picture taken in 1927 supporters make their way to see another big game.

30s, with Edinburgh's Meadowbank as an alternative. An abiding memory of those summer days was the steam roadroller lumbering round the red ash track between events to flatten the running surface.

★ ★ ★ ★ ★

CELTIC and Rangers came out of the hat together in the Scottish Cup semi-final draw in 1925 and clashed at Hampden for the first time since 1909. The match itself was a one-sided affair, with Celtic thrashing their great rivals 5-0. The real significance of the occasion lay in the crowd – 101,714 spectators watched the match, the first six-figure attendance for a club match. It was a foretaste of great occasions to come.

The Hoops went on to lift the trophy, coming from behind to beat Dundee 2-1 in the final thanks to an incredible equalising goal from Patsy Gallagher – who somersaulted over the line with the ball jammed between his ankles – and a late winner from Jimmy McGrory.

A week before that final, Scotland had lined up at Hampden to face England knowing that victory would bring yet another International Championship and a 100 per cent record in that season's tournament. With English clubs content to release players for their own national side but not for the Scots, it was left to an all-Scottish League side to do battle for their country.

While the big names of the day such as Hughie Gallagher, Alan Morton and Davie Meiklejohn were present, the absence of the Anglos allowed some unlikely others such as Ayr United's Philip McCloy and David Morris of Raith Rovers– who actually captained the team – to play their part in a convincing Scottish win.

The victory belonged to Gallagher above all. The Airdrie striker scored both goals in the 2-0

WINNING THE BLUES: Celtic keeper John Thomson tips the ball over the bar, far right, to foil a Rangers attack in the 1928 Scottish Cup Final. More than 100,000 fans crammed into Hampden Park to watch the action, including some youngsters who clambered over the wall to get into the ground.

victory that sparked off a transfer frenzy among the leading English clubs. Within 10 months, seven of this team had been transferred south and only the Old Firm players remained with their clubs.

The Scottish Cup found a new home in 1926 – Paisley – as St Mirren avenged their 1908 final defeat by beating Celtic 2-0 in front of a crowd of 98,620. However, 1926 was a watershed. Ten of the following 11 Scottish Cups were destined for either Ibrox or Parkhead.

Just as in 1925, Celtic had to come from behind before securing the trophy by beating East Fife 3-1. The Fifers – sixth in Division Two – made a contest of it and the expected "barrowload" of goals didn't materialise. East Fife not only enjoyed their day, they learned from it.

If Celtic were experienced in Hampden triumph, so too was the national side. When they played England in front of 111,214 spectators on April 2, 1927, they did so with a record that was the envy of the world. Scotland

NET PROFIT: Crowds flocked to Hampden in 1927 to watch the Wimbledon singles champion Suzanne Lenglen play an exhibition tennis match. The elegant French woman caused quite a stir with her "revealing" outfit!

had won their last eight home internationals, seven of them without conceding a goal, and were undefeated in 10 matches. It had been seven years since they had lost to England. In fact, the last time the white shirts had won in Glasgow, both the Kaiser and the Czar were sitting happily on their thrones. Amazingly, England had never won at the third Hampden Park.

England were forced to play with centre-half Hill as a "passenger" out on the wing and a goal from Morton to cheer the home fans, it looked like business as usual. But up popped a little-known English debutant from Everton by the name of William Ralph Dean. The youngster equalised then scored the winner with under 120 seconds left to play.

The title was shared with England but Scotland's long run of home mastery had come to an end. This was England's first win on Scottish soil since 1904 and their first ever at the new home of Scottish football. His name may not have been famous then, but the exploits of "Dixie" Dean have echoed across the generations ever since. One of the greatest scorers of all time announced his arrival at Hampden Park that April afternoon. Twelve months later, Scotland gained ample revenge with a 5-1 win at Wembley achieved by a side that has gone down in history as the Wembley Wizards.

★ ★ ★ ★ ★

ALTHOUGH the sport is associated with the more genteel surroundings of London's SW19, crowds flocked to Hampden in 1927 to watch tennis. The reason was the presence of the sport's first female superstar, Suzanne Lenglen. The elegant French player had won the Wimbledon singles title six times and her dress – revealing forearms and ankles – was the sensation of its time. Lenglen had turned professional in 1926 and in those days that meant world tours and exhibition matches. Her entourage pulled up at Hampden on July 12, 1927, and, on a specially-prepared green-painted wooden surface in front of the South Stand, she whipped her English opponent, Mrs Vivian Dewhurst, who was described as being of "athletic build", 6-2 6-0 in just 20 minutes. The 10,000 spectators then saw a three-set men's singles match between Howard Kinsey and Karl Kozelun. A further novelty was the umpire's use of a microphone, which broadcast his decisions via 12 loudspeakers dotted round the ground.

★ ★ ★ ★ ★

WHEN Rangers lined up to face Celtic at Hampden in the Scottish Cup Final of 1928 it had been a full quarter of a century since the world's oldest trophy had last taken up residence at Ibrox. So great was the interest in the game that a new Scottish Cup record attendance was set as 118,115 lined up on the slopes to watch the old enemies do battle.

Rangers went ahead 10 minutes after the break when captain Davie Meiklejohn slotted home a penalty. Midway through the half, Bob McPhail pounced on a fumble by Celtic keeper John Thomson to scramble a second goal then a 25-yarder from right-winger Sandy Archibald screamed into the net. Archibald lashed in a fourth near the end to send the Rangers support home ecstatic. Almost 40 years after the foundation of the Scottish League, this was the Ibrox club's first League and Cup "double".

In the next decade, manager Bill Struth's Rangers dominated Scottish football in a manner unsurpassed until the arrival of Jock Stein at Parkhead. Hampden became a second home for their fans.

But it wasn't only the presence of the Old Firm that guaranteed large crowds. A 1928 quarter-final tie between Queen's Park and Partick Thistle attracted 65,000, who saw the Spiders reach the last four, where they lost to Celtic. Another massive attendance – 114,708, the first six-figure crowd for any club game other than an Old Firm match – descended on the 1929 cup final, forcing the gates to close well before kick-off. And the match was astonishing in more ways than one. Holders Rangers were on course for another "double" if they could beat Kilmarnock, a mid-table team who were hampered by injury.

The scene seemed set for an easy Rangers' triumph but the script was torn up after just 16 minutes. After intense pressure, Rangers earned a penalty but a salmon-like leap from Killie keeper Sam Clemie denied Tully Craig from the spot. Three minutes into the second half, Killie left-winger John Aitken pounced on a mis-hit clearance to put his team ahead. With 12 minutes remaining, inside-left Jimmy Williamson put Killie 2-0 ahead. To compound the Ibrox misery, Jock Buchanan received his marching orders in the dying minutes – the first player to be sent off in a Scottish Cup Final.

Just seven days later, Scotland lined up against England at Hampden in a match that first drew the world's attention to two locally-produced phenomena – the Hampden Swirl and the Hampden Roar.

A victory would give the Scots another International Championship with a 100 per cent record but the crowd of 110,512 witnessed a disappointing match in which Scotland were reduced to 10 men in the first half when Alex Jackson had to go off with a dislocated elbow – there were no substitutes in those days. As the game meandered towards a goalless draw, the Scots won a 90th-minute corner. Up stepped Cheyne to take the kick.

He put the ball into the air, at which point the breeze which tended to "swirl" around the vast bowl made its presence felt. It sent the ball swerving and dipping past bewildered England keeper John Hacking and into the net. It was the last kick of the match. The roar that greeted Cheyne's goal was so loud, it was heard a mile away at the Victoria Infirmary, where Jackson reputedly sat up in his hospital bed and shouted: "Scotland's won!"

A few weeks earlier, another set of Scotland's internationalists had also shown the door to their English counterparts at Hampden – New Lesser Hampden to be precise – but the game wasn't football. Scotland's men's hockey XI achieved a rare victory over the Auld Enemy thanks to goals from Brooks, McLeod and Knight.

CUP HERO: Celtic's Jimmy McGrory, seen here in action in the 1933 Final against Motherwell, scored the goal which dumped Dundee in the 1925 Final at Hampden.

MATCH DAY: An aerial shot of Hampden shows another big crowd cheering on their favourites in the mid 1960s.

60

ALEC'S ACE: The famous Hampden swirl confuses England goalkeeper John Hacking and Alec Cheyne's corner kick lands up in the back of the net to give Scotland a famous victory in 1929.

Chapter 4

The Creation of a Modern Colosseum

DURING the 1930s, Hampden achieved a status which would have seemed unthinkable to its founding fathers. It became the largest and most impressive arena on the planet – a modern Colosseum, setting records which still stand to this day.

The stadium was the only one which came close to accommodating the incredible masses of Scots who had grown addicted to the game of football. No matter how big its capacity became, there were still thousands who were left frustrated at its gates as the "Sold Out" signs went up.

Rangers were keen to make up for their wilderness years in the cup and paid no fewer than four visits to the National Stadium in 1930. First, a solitary strike from Bob McPhail was good enough to see off Queen's Park in the opening round of the cup watched by 95,722 – the largest crowd ever at a Spiders match. Another massive Hampden gate – 92,084 – saw Rangers overwhelm Hearts 4-1 in the semi-final and then 107,475 saw a closely-fought, but goalless, encounter between Gers and Partick Thistle in the final.

Four days later, a new British midweek record attendance was set as 103,686 watched the replay. Despite losing Alan Morton through injury after just 15 minutes, Rangers took the lead through James Marshall but John Torbet levelled for Thistle in 72 minutes. With four minutes left, Tully Craig tried a spectacular lob that beat keeper John Jackson, who was unsighted by the sun to send the cup back to Ibrox.

Twelve months later, the outstanding provincial team of inter-war football – Motherwell – made their cup final debut against Celtic. The Lanarkshire contingent in the crowd of 104,863 was given plenty to cheer when goals from Stevenson and McMenemy put the Claret and Ambers ahead after only 21 minutes. But with just eight minutes remaining, Jimmy McGrory threw Celtic a lifeline. Even so, the trophy still looked like 'Well's until

FOILED: More than 102,000 people jammed into Hampden in 1933 to see Celtic captain Jimmy McStay lift the Scottish Cup after a 1-0 win against Motherwell.

Bobby Thomson punted a last-minute cross into the box and Motherwell centre-half Alan Craig headed into his own net.

Stunned 'Well could scarcely believe a match that had been in the bag for so long could end in a draw. The disbelief still haunted them when the replay got under way – and the Hoops were 3-1 ahead by half-time. Although Motherwell fought all the way, Celtic ran out 4-2 winners. It was the start of a 20-year trail of cup heartbreak for the Steelmen.

The records continued to tumble. A new world record crowd of 129,810 squeezed in for the 1931 clash with England, who arrived at Hampden in the unaccustomed position of being strong favourites. While they could pick their strongest team, a new Football League ban on the release of players meant the Scots were restricted to a home-based side.

But with an hour played, English keeper Harry Hibbs dropped the ball at the feet of Motherwell's George Stevenson, who promptly netted to give the Scots an unlikely lead. Two minutes later, the Hampden Roar could be heard at full blast as Jimmy McGrory bagged the second. Buoyed by the backing of their fans, the Scots held out comfortably to record a famous victory against the odds.

But for two legends it was their Hampden farewell. Alan Morton, who had started out playing his club football at the ground, played his final home match in a Scotland strip – although he managed three more caps away from home to establish a record total of 31 appearances, a tally unmatched until after the Second World War.

Tragically, it was also the last international appearance for young Celtic goalkeeper John

Thomson, who died following an accidental collision with Sam English of Rangers in a league match at Ibrox in September 1931.

★ ★ ★ ★ ★

MOTHERWELL, who made amends for their cup failure by winning the Scottish League in 1932, returned to Hampden in the cup to knock out Queen's Park in front of 56,000, then eliminated Celtic before losing to Rangers. The Ibrox team faced 1929 conquerors Kilmarnock in the final and, with six-figure gates now the norm, the crowd of 111,982 caused barely a raised eyebrow. The sides drew 1-1 but the Glasgow side won the replay 3-0 in front of a record midweek crowd of 105,695.

It took Rangers three games – two of them at Hampden – to overcome Queen's Park in the 1933 competition but dreams of a second successive cup success were dashed by defeat at Rugby Park in the next round. Once again the finalists were familiar faces. Few among the 102,339 crowd could claim that this Celtic v Motherwell encounter lived long in their memory. Jimmy McGrory's goal early in the second half settled a drab affair for Celtic.

Another world record crowd – 136,259 – saw the 1933 match against England. Scotland were captained by Queen's Park's Bob Gillespie, the last amateur to skipper the national team. We say "national" but this was more of a Glasgow select. Celtic and Rangers provided three players each, Queen's Park had two and Partick Thistle's John Jackson was in goal. Right-back Andy Anderson of Hearts and left-winger "Dally" Duncan from Derby County were the only "outsiders".

The result, a 2-1 win over the English thanks to two goals from Jimmy McGrory, says much for the strength of football in Scotland, and Glasgow in particular, at that time.

A challenge of a different sort was faced later that year when foreign opposition visited for the first time. The "Wunderteam" of Austria, coached by the Hugo Meisl and led on the pitch by the legendary Matthias Sindelar, were highly regarded on the continent and, of course, had thrashed Scotland 5-0 in Vienna in 1931. A crowd of 62,000 saw an entertaining 2-2 draw which featured a fascinating contrast of styles. Motherwell's Willie McFadyen caused consternation in the Austrian ranks with his shoulder charges – perfectly legal here but frowned upon on the continent. Sindelar was known as "Die Papierene" – the Man of Paper – because of his style which had been inspired by the Scotch Professors.

The year 1933 also saw Hampden witness its biggest-ever crowd. Nearly

CAPTAIN FANTASTIC:
Queen's Park's Bob Gillespie was the last amateur to skipper the Scotland team.

CROWD PULLER: Hampden's biggest crowd was for the Boys' Brigade Jubilee Conventicle. 130,000 packed into the ground and another 100,000 waited outside to join in the psalm singing.

69

FOILED: Hamilton keeper Jimmy Morgan punches clear as Bobby Main of Rangers threatens in the 1935 Final.

ACTION STATIONS: Simpson of Scotland tussles with England's Geldard in the 1935 International at Hampden.

a quarter of a million turned up on Sunday, September 11 – and they weren't even there for a football match. The Glasgow-founded Boys' Brigade had grown from humble beginnings in 1883 to spread round the globe and chose Hampden to celebrate its Jubilee year. With 130,000 inside and more than 100,000 outside, the BB Conventicle was the largest open-air religious service ever seen in the UK and the culmination of a week of events in the city that concluded with psalm-singing vigorous enough to be heard over a mile away.

Hampden has witnessed many tense Scottish Cup Finals but 1934's was not one of them. The most surprising aspect of the game between Rangers and St Mirren was that it took 36 minutes for the fragile Paisley defence to concede a goal. After that, the net bulged at regular intervals as Gers ran out 5-0 winners in front of 113,430 fans.

After attracting a combined total of more than 200,000 to see them dispose of Hearts in their semi final and replay, Rangers took on Hamilton in the 1935 final but a certain level of fatigue had clearly set in among the fans and less than 90,000 turned out. The Academicals put up a spirited fight but the Ibrox men edged a 2-1 win, despite missing a penalty.

Dally Duncan netted twice to give Scotland a 2-0 win over England in that year's Home International and, unusually, the sides squared up again later the same year. In a fundraiser for the King George V Jubilee Trust Fund, more than 55,000 contributed their pennies to good causes and had the added pleasure of seeing a 4-2 home win.

Rangers were back for yet another Scottish

Cup Final in 1936 when they faced fellow Glaswegians Third Lanark. Bob McPhail had the ball in the net within 90 seconds and the Gers support eagerly anticipated a rout. Thirds recovered so well, however, that Rangers keeper Jerry Dawson was given much of the credit for his side's victory.

A third successive Scottish Cup victory was a fitting Hampden farewell for Ibrox skipper Davie Meiklejohn. On the other hand, Thirds said a sad goodbye to Hampden – at least on Scottish Cup Final business. The Cathkin club never again appeared at the ground in Scottish football's biggest event.

But 1937 was Hampden Park's wonder year. Major ground improvements included the erection of the funny, crook-shaped North Stand perched on stilts at the top of the terracing. The official capacity was now calculated to be a staggering 183,388. Prompted by the local authority, the SFA agreed to issue "only" 150,000 tickets for their games but attendance records set that year are still unmatched anywhere in Europe and surpassed only at Rio de Janeiro's Maracana Stadium.

The Scottish Cup Final on April 24th, 1937, attracted 147,365 paying customers with 20,000 stranded outside when the gates were closed 15 minutes before kick-off. It was the largest attendance for any club match in the world. The contestants were Celtic, aiming for their 15th success, and Aberdeen, who were appearing in their very first final. Celtic took an early lead, the Dons quickly equalised but Buchan scored a killer strike for the Hoops after 70 minutes. Jimmy McGrory, another of the game's inter-war legends, collected his fourth winner's medal to bring down the curtain on his Hampden playing career.

A week before the final, an even bigger crowd had assembled. The official 149,415 attendance for the match against England was the largest anywhere in the world at that time – and at least a further 20,000 got through or over the turnstiles. Yet the game was of little significance. Wales had won the Home Nations title and pride was all that was at stake. But pride is more than enough where Scotland and England are concerned. In addition to star names like Britton, Hapgood and Carter, the English also had the incomparable winger Stanley Matthews. But Scotland had their stars, too. Jimmy Delaney, Tommy Walker and Dally Duncan were all in tremendous form and Bob McPhail, nearing the end of his career, could still terrorise defences.

England dominated the first half and Freddie Steele put them ahead close to the interval. The second half, though, was to provide the stuff of legend. An imperious English XI strode out early for the restart but were made

HEADLINE NEWS: How the Sunday Mail reported the 1937 final. A huge 147,365 people saw the action and another 20,000 were stranded outside the ground.

SUNDAY MAIL, APRIL 25, 1937—Page .9

FINAL OF FINESSE AND FRENZY
Britain's Record Cup Crowd Was Fascinated

Verdict: "Celtic Better Team"
By "BEDOUIN"

BUCHAN'S WINNING GOAL A MASTERPIECE

That Amazing Kennaway Save— Was Beynon Surprised!

Handing Over The Cup To Celtic

CELTIC 2 ABERDEEN 1

CROWD PLEASERS: Celtic's Chic Geatons swings in a cross despite a challenge from Mills of Aberdeen in the 1937 Final. Below: Jimmy Delaney's winners' medal.

to wait by their opponents. When the Scots finally re-emerged, it was to a wall of deafening noise as their "twelfth man" – the Hampden Roar – came into play.

Inspired by the noise, Frank O'Donnell equalised just two minutes after the restart and it was then one-way traffic towards Vic Woodley in the English goal. Then, 10 minutes from time, 31-year-old McPhail unleashed a 15-yard drive past Woodley to give Scotland the lead. And with two minutes left, he headed home to wrap up a 3-1 victory. Afterwards, Matthews paid tribute to the crowd, declaring they had been the inspiration behind the Scottish triumph. McPhail couldn't resist a dig at the Auld Enemy and, when one fan complained there had been no room to move on the terracing, Bob replied: "You should have been where I was. I had plenty of room."

Everyone in the massive crowd should have savoured the moment. It would be 25 long years before Scotland savoured again the sweet taste of a win over England in an official game at Hampden.

The celebrations to mark the coronation of George VI included a huge rally at Hampden in May 1937. Around 40,000 exuberant spectators saw an athletics programme, presentations of physical culture, children's displays, bands, fireworks and the inevitable football match – a Glasgow select overcoming their Edinburgh counterparts 2-0.

Four years after the trailblazing Austrians, Czechoslovakia arrived at Mount Florida in December 1937. They contained five of the team that had taken hosts Italy to extra time in the 1934 World Cup Final. Yet it seemed the

FANTASTIC FOR FIFERS: Laird of East Fife stops Kilmarnock's McGrogan in the epic 1938 Hampden Final, right, and McLeod celebrates after giving the Methil men the lead in the first game, far right.

Scots were treating their guests with less than total respect. Incredibly, the selectors treated the game against the World Cup finalists as a trial match. Imagine that happening today! Scotland handed debuts to six players – a risky strategy, as the Czechs had narrowly lost 5-4 to England just prior to the Hampden match – but it all came together amazingly well. Andy Black of Hearts put the Scots in front within a minute. The London pairing of McCulloch of Brentford and Buchanan from Chelsea made it 3-0 at half-time. McCulloch scored again in the second half and a strike from Rangers' Kinnear gave the home side a comfortable 5-0 win. It was a marvellous result that pleased the 41,000 crowd but continental football still counted for little in UK eyes in those days. Only Black out of the six debutants ever played for Scotland again.

★ ★ ★ ★ ★

JIMMY McGRORY may have been finished with Hampden as a player but he was soon back as a manager. After taking over at Kilmarnock, Scotland's greatest-ever scorer led his new charges on an epic cup run. They vanquished his beloved Celtic at Parkhead and demolished local rivals Ayr United 5-0 at Somerset Park before ousting Rangers 4-3 in an epic semi-final at Hampden. After just four months in the hot seat, McGrory was back at Hampden for the 1938 final.

Only Second Division East Fife stood between Killie and a third success – but the match was a huge

BONNIE FOR CLYDE: Dougie Wallace, Willie Martin and David Noble parade the Scottish Cup after their 1939 win.

disappointment. McLeod gave East Fife the lead in 17 minutes but the Ayrshire side levelled through McAvoy eight minutes later. There were few thrills and no more goals.

For the first time at Hampden, the replay crowd beat the first game's and this time fans were treated to an epic. The Second Leaguers again took the lead in 15 minutes through McKerrell. Four minutes later, Benny Thomson equalised with a penalty and Felix McGrogan put Killie ahead before the interval with a fine solo goal. McLeod made it 2-2 with an overhead kick in 57 minutes to take the game into extra-time. In the 110th minute, East Fife's Miller seized on a poor clearance to put his side ahead and McKerrell's second goal sealed the tie four minutes later to take the cup to Fife for the first time. With the exception of then non-league Queen's Park in 1893, East Fife became the first, and so far only, side to win the trophy from outwith the country's top division.

If East Fife provided the fairytale story of the Scottish Cup then Motherwell's record was the stuff of horror stories. In 1939, they were back for their third final in eight years. But the heartbreak of defeat didn't get any easier. With their great days behind them, the Steelmen were just another average mid-table side – as were their opponents Clyde, who were the only one of the six Glasgow clubs never to have won the Scottish Cup up till then.

With the wind against them, Clyde took the lead after half an hour and withstood a barrage of 'Well attacks. Five minutes after the break, a Motherwell defender went down in a challenge and keeper Murray gently rolled the ball towards team-mate Blair for the free-kick – but the referee had not blown his whistle. Clyde's centre-forward Martin cheekily trapped the ball and shot under the keeper to make it 2-0. Motherwell were a beaten side and Clyde added two more goals before the final whistle. Bully Wee fans in the crowd of 94,799 were ecstatic and the victorious players were met with adulation by thousands along a route from Rutherglen to Bridgeton Cross. Many fans were so anxious to greet their heroes that they left Hampden well before the end of the game.

It would be a long time before the supporters of any other club were allowed a similar celebration. Thanks to Adolf Hitler, the Scottish Cup remained in Clyde's possession for the next eight years.

The international against England in April 1939 was the first at Hampden since the Czech game 16 months earlier and was also the last official international for more than seven years. Another amazing crowd – 149,269 –

STAR MAN: England's wonder winger Stanley Matthews takes on the Scottish defence at Hampden Park – the ground where he made his international debut.

PREPARING FOR WAR: Policemen wearing steel helmets and carrying gas masks parade past Hampden's North Stand.

watched the match in torrential conditions. After 20 minutes, Preston's Jimmy Dougall put the home side ahead. But this England team was made of stern stuff. It contained players such as Eddie Hapgood, Stan Cullis, Joe Mercer, Tommy Lawton and Stanley Matthews, who were among the best in the business. They equalised midway through the second half with a superb drive from Huddersfield's Albert Beasley. Two minutes from time Matthews beat two defenders and produced a perfect cross for Lawton to head past Jerry Dawson in the Scotland goal.

Fifteen days later, a National Service demonstration was staged at Hampden. It was a dummy run then but most present believed the drill carried out that day would shortly be re-enacted for real. The outbreak of war in September 1939 resulted in the suspension of organised football. But once the fear of immediate air attack on heavily-attended grounds receded, the Government and the SFA began to look upon the game in a more favourable light.

At first, friendlies were organised away from military installations, munitions factories and shipbuilding areas, then came Regional Leagues. The Scottish Cup went into hibernation for the duration of the conflict, so the League organised its own Emergency War Cup knock-out tournament on a two-leg basis.

Hampden staged one semi-final, in which Rangers overcame Motherwell to earn a final spot against Second Division Dundee United.

May 1940 witnessed some of the darkest days in history as much of Europe fell under the heel of Nazi tyranny. Even as Winston

DUMMY RUN: Hampden Park was the scene of a National Service demonstration in the spring of 1939. It was preparation for the war which broke out in September that year.

Churchill was vowing to "fight them on the beaches", it is strange to think that football, and the lure of Hampden, still held such a mesmerising effect on so many Scots.

The Home Office limited attendances at matches to 50 per cent of capacity, so the 75,000 who saw Jimmy Smith's goal send the wartime trophy to Ibrox represented a full house. Later in May, a similar figure attended the match against England that ended in a 1-1 draw… and a hail of boos directed at the referee for disallowing a late "winner" for the Scots.

The Parashots – the forerunner of the LDV and the Home Guard – set up a post at New Lesser Hampden in 1940 and a government official turned up with an order for both pitches to be ploughed up and used to plant vegetables. Queen's Park said that the order did not affect sports grounds and sat tight. Nothing was ever heard again.

Wartime and conscription meant that team line-ups were in a state of constant flux, with many top names turning out for clubs close to their barracks. As a result, Stanley Matthews, the greatest player of his era, pulled on a Rangers jersey as a guest of the club in the Charity Cup Final of May 1941, won 3-0 by the Ibrox side against Partick Thistle.

That year also saw the introduction of the forerunner of the League Cup. The Southern League Cup was established on the basis of four groups of four. Around 65,000 fans saw Rangers and Hearts draw 1-1 in the final, with 60,000 watching a terrific replay. The sides remained deadlocked at 2-2 with five minutes remaining but the Light Blues struck twice to lift the trophy. The Ibrox men were edged out 3-2 at Hampden by Hibs in a thrilling final of a new competition, the Summer Cup, but the crowd was a poor 36,734.

It was probably just as well for Scotland that the wartime games at Hampden against England are regarded as unofficial. With few exceptions, the home side came off badly – often very badly.

The clash in May 1941 was typical. An Alex Venters goal helped earn some respect as England coasted to a 3-1 victory. But a year later, on April 18th, 1942, 91,000 supporters cheered a famous Scottish victory. Jock Dodds scored a hat-trick and Bill Shankly and debutant Billy Liddell weighed in with a goal apiece as Scotland narrowly won 5-4.

Rangers picked up both club trophies on offer in 1941-42 – Morton lost 1-0 to a Torry Gillick goal in the Southern League Cup final then in July 1942, Rangers took the Summer Cup from Hibs due to sheer luck, calling correctly as a coin was tossed to decide the winners after 120 goalless minutes.

★ ★ ★ ★ ★

ON October 31, 1942, the 39th anniversary of Hampden's first game, strange new sports made their debuts at the ground as American forces in the West of Scotland put on a display of softball, baseball and American football – all received with mystification by the locals.

Some American imports were more popular than others. The world-famous actor Edward G. Robinson visited Hampden in 1942. Robinson had emigrated from Romania aged 10 when his family fled from persecution and he delivered a series of anti-fascist broadcasts and pep talks on the BBC. Edward G who had gained fame as a film gangster greeted the cheers of the Hampden crowd with: "Pipe down youse bums or youse are gonna get it."

Even more popular than Robinson was boxer Jackie Paterson. In June 1943, more than 60,000 fight fans turned up at Hampden to see him take on World Flyweight champion Peter Kane – a Lancastrian blacksmith who had won his title at Liverpool's Anfield stadium in 1938. Kane had fought twice (one defeat and a draw) against Scotland's first world champion Benny Lynch and was well fancied to beat Paterson. But the fight was short, sharp and brutal. Precisely one minute and one second of the first round had elapsed before Kane was counted out and Scotland had a new world champion.

Paterson held on to his flyweight crown for four years and even moved up to bantamweight, where he won the British, Commonwealth and European titles. The Scot was stripped of his flyweight crowns after twice failing to make a defence against Hawaiian Dado Marino in 1947 before the authorities relented and allowed him the dignity of losing them in the ring against Rinty Monaghan. Paterson had lost all his titles by the time he stepped

into the Hampden ring for one last hurrah against world bantamweight champion Manuel Ortiz in October 1949. It's a sign of how gruelling the fight game was at that time that this was Paterson's 89th pro contest in 11 years, only two months after his last bout. Ortiz was fighting for the 112th time, just three weeks after his last contest.

After 10 weary, energy-sapping rounds, the Mexican-American won on points. It was the last Hampden fight of the 20th century. For Paterson, there were just three more contests – all lost – in a career and life in sharp decline.

PIPE DOWN: Film Star Edward G

★ ★ ★ ★ ★

AFTER their cup win on the toss of a coin in 1942, Rangers retained the Southern League Cup

OVER AND OUT: Peter Kane is counted out in the first round against Scottish boxer Jackie Paterson (opposite page).

by another unusual method in 1943. Their clash with Falkirk ended 1-1 but Gers kept the trophy because they had won 11 corners to the Bairns' three. On July 10th, the Summer Cup found a new home when St Mirren beat the Ibrox side by a single goal.

A dismal Scotland were taken apart 4-0 by England at Hampden in April 1943 in front of the first six-figure wartime crowd. At least Scotland made a fight of it at Hampden the next year. A goal from Jimmy Caskie and an own goal from Stan Cullis were the Scottish strikes in a narrow 3-2 defeat. One consolation came in the crowd figure of 133,000 – a record for a wartime fixture.

The Juniors returned to Hampden in 1943 when Rob Roy beat Bedlay in the semi-final of the Junior Cup. The Kirkintilloch team followed it up in the final by beating Benburb after a replay. It was the start of a long relationship between the Junior Cup and the national stadium. Over the next few seasons, several semi-finals were played there and Rob Roy's victory marked the first of 39 successive Junior Cup Finals at Hampden.

Just weeks before the D-Day invasion of Normandy, a crowd of 63,000 saw a goal-less Southern League Cup Final between Rangers and Hibs in May 1944 – but this time the corner kick count went in the Edinburgh side's favour. The Old Firm opted out of the Summer Cup but the contest continued with yet another novel way found to separate teams after a drawn game.

The semi-final between Clyde and Morton ended 3-3 after extra time with both teams having taken 15 corners. Rather than toss a coin, goal average in previous games was taken into account and Clyde were declared victors. In the final, Motherwell exacted a measure of revenge for their 1939 cup final defeat with a 1-0 win over Clyde.

Rangers regained the Southern League Cup in 1944-45, beating Motherwell 2-1 in an entertaining final on May 12, 1945 – four days after VE Day. Partick Thistle also picked up a rare trophy, beating Hibs 2-0 in the Summer Cup Final. But the disappointing Hampden crowd of 27,996

84

BACK ON TRACK: Scotland were crushed 3-1 by England in 1941 but recovered to beat the Auld Enemy a year later in a nine-goal thriller. Beattie and Steele are pictured above during the first clash (See Page 81).

killed off any chance of the tournament surviving into peacetime. A massive 130,000-strong crowd was left bitterly disappointed when England came calling. Trailing 3-1, Matt Busby missed a penalty and the English won by an embarrassingly easy 6-1.

Tommy Bogan of Hibs made his solitary Scotland appearance but was taken off injured shortly after kick-off without having touched the ball.

In some aspects, however, wartime football was more progressive than its peacetime counterpart. Bogan was replaced by Leslie Johnstone of Clyde – fully 20 years before substitutes were legalised in Scottish football.

★ ★ ★ ★ ★

THE 1945-46 season was last "unofficial" wartime one and brought a new name to the attention of the trophy engravers.

Aberdeen won their first-ever national trophy when a last-minute goal by left-half Taylor gave them a 3-2 win over Rangers in the misnamed Southern League Cup Final in front of an incredible crowd of 133,000.

The last word on official wartime trophies lay with Rangers, who beat Hibs 3-0 in the Victory Cup showdown on June 15th.

November 1945 heralded the first signs of a refreshing new approach from the authorities as Wales arrived at Mount Florida.

Goals from Willie Waddell and Jock Dodds gave the Scots a 2-0 win, while the crowd of 97,000 justified those who argued it made little sense to restrict the

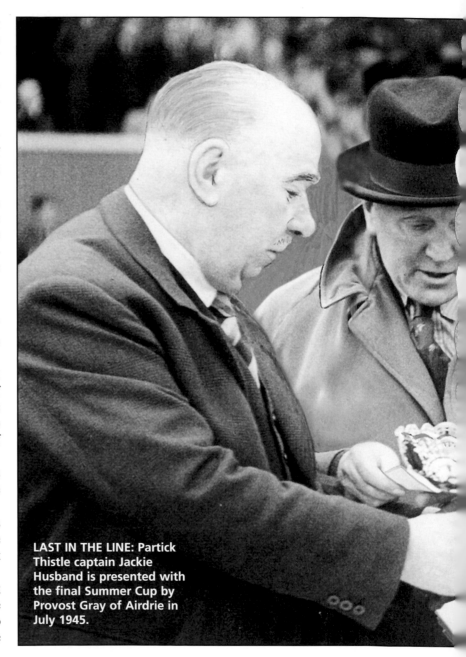

LAST IN THE LINE: Partick Thistle captain Jackie Husband is presented with the final Summer Cup by Provost Gray of Airdrie in July 1945.

biggest ground in the world to one international every two years.

For the next 25 years, virtually all Scotland games were played at Hampden. In the post-war boom, it was the only ground big enough to cope.

On the evening of Christmas day, 1945, fire swept through the centre-west section of the main stand, destroying the press box and seriously damaging the boardroom and administrative offices. Irreplaceable records and paperwork went up in flames.

Belgium paid their first visit to Hampden in January 1946 and surprised the 46,000 crowd by putting on a good show. They led by 2-1 into the final minute when a Jimmy Delaney penalty saved both the Scots' blushes and their unbeaten home record against continental opposition.

Delaney was the hero again against England in front of 139,468, scoring the only goal of the game as Scotland helped banish the blues of six successive defeats from the Auld Enemy.

Switzerland were next, and although they stunned the 113,000 crowd by taking the lead early on, two goals from Billy Liddell and the inevitable strike from Delaney gave the home side a 3-1 victory.

These games, however, were all regarded as "unofficial" by the SFA. But as the world sought to recover from the ravages of the deadliest war in human history, football was king.

Of all the grounds in all the cities in all the world, Hampden stood proudly above them all. The modern Colosseum.

BURNED OUT: The damage caused by the fire which raged through Hampden's main stand on Christmas Day 1945.

PROUD CAPTAINS: Matt Busby, of Scotland, and England's Joe Mercer lead out their teams for the 1945 International.

Chapter 5

Football Unites the Country as Peace Returns

NOVEMBER 27th, 1946, was the day that peacetime football returned as Northern Ireland made their inaugural appearance at Hampden. Sadly, the occasion wasn't marked by a better game. Both teams hit the woodwork and the Scots slightly shaded the play but the match finished goalless. The astounding size of the crowd was the main talking point. Normally a game against the Irish might attract around 40,000 or so. This one was watched by 98,776. Football was back and no mistake! For Hampden Park, the good times were about to roll.

In many ways the following quarter of a century was Hampden's Golden Age. It was an era when six-figure gates were the norm – not just for the Old Firm and Scotland matches but for Motherwell v Dundee and St Mirren v Aberdeen. It wasn't just internationals that saw Hampden's fixture list increase. The Southern League Cup was revamped to include all league teams and renamed the Scottish League Cup. To the surprise of no one bar, perhaps, their final opponents from Aberdeen, the first name engraved on the new trophy in 1947 was that of Rangers. But the new competition quickly gained the reputation as one where the smaller clubs could win silverware. East Fife repeated their pre-war Scottish Cup exploits and, as a lower division side, won the second League Cup with Davie Duncan scoring the first final hat-trick in the competition.

Another 'B' Division team from Fife – Raith Rovers – reached the final in 1949 but lost to a Rangers side on their way to a historic first domestic "treble". Now a top-flight team, East Fife came back to win the silver again, this time beating lower league Dunfermline in an all-Fife final. And the following season, Motherwell at long last claimed Hampden success, beating Hibs 3-0 in the 1950-51 final. Dundee were another side to taste Hampden success for the first time when they beat Rangers 3-2 the following season and the Dens men repeated their success the next year, winning 2-0 against a Kilmarnock team that became the fourth 'B' Division side to reach

THIRD MEN: The Press Box seems about to fall off the roof of the South Stand during the 1959 League Cup Final between Third Lanark and Hearts. Here, Thirds keeper Robertson cuts out a cross.

the final. The competition reached new heights in 1953-54 when East Fife won for a record third time. They seemed to be strolling to victory, having gone 2-0 ahead against Partick Thistle in the opening 10 minutes. But Thistle came roaring back in the second half to level the game before Charlie Christie scored from outside the box with just three minutes to play. For Thistle, this was the beginning of Hampden heartbreak in the competition that would continue for almost two decades.

The next season, Motherwell faced Hearts in the final in front of more than 55,000. The Jambos won 4-2, thanks chiefly to a Willie Bauld hat-trick, to lift their first major trophy for almost 50 years.

Celtic had made little impact in this competition but finally came good in 1956-57, although it took them two games to see off Partick Thistle. The attendance for the replay was just 31,126.

In the 1957-58 League Cup, lowly Brechin City went on a superb run which brought them to Hampden in the semi-finals. But their dreams of glory were dashed by Rangers, who won at a canter. Waiting for them in the final were the holders Celtic. It was the first Old Firm League Cup Final. It was also the most sensational.

The attendance of 82,293 was low by Old Firm standards but the players approached the match as if their lives depended on it. Celtic twice hit the woodwork before Sammy Wilson put them ahead. Neilly Mochan drove in a second goal just before the break, then Billy McPhail scored after the interval. Billy Simpson briefly restored Rangers hopes with a goal to make it 3-1 but McPhail scored again to restore the three-goal margin. Mochan added another and McPhail secured his hat-trick before being knocked over in the box in the final minute.

Willie Fernie despatched the penalty to complete an incredible game and make the final score 7-1 to Celtic.

SEVENTH HEAVEN: Celtic's scorers Willie Fernie, Billy McPhail, Neil Mochan and Sammy Wilson, above left, celebrate the 7-1 defeat of Rangers in 1957, which made headlines all over Britain.

Beforehand, there were few who would have dared to predict a Celtic victory, let alone one of this magnitude.

Hearts arrived at Hampden for the 1958-59 final as reigning league champions. They cruised to a 5-1 victory over Partick for their second League Cup victory but poor Thistle had now lost three finals in five years.

The only Glasgow side to make a cup final appearance in 1959 were Third Lanark, who faced holders Hearts in the 1959-60 League Cup Final. Matt Gray put Thirds ahead after just two minutes but two goals in the space of a minute from Johnny Hamilton and Alex Young secured victory for the Edinburgh side. Seven years later, Third Lanark disappeared amid accusations of mismanagement.

★ ★ ★ ★ ★

THE Scottish Cup retained its majestic allure throughout the post-war years. Travel was still difficult for 1947's competition and the SFA did everything possible to avoid replays. Hibernian and Motherwell were under

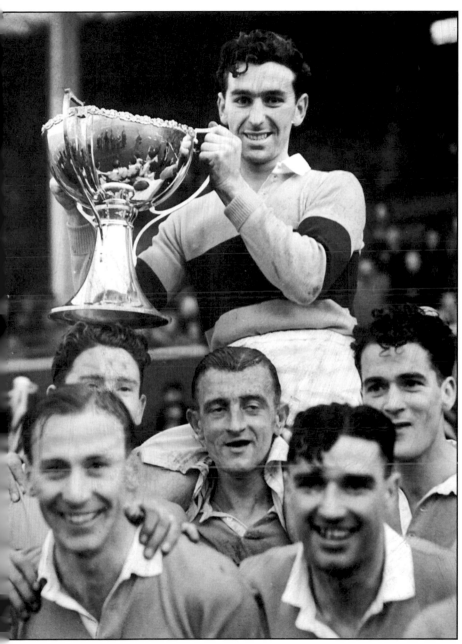

instructions to "get a result no matter what" in their Hampden semi-final. Level at 1-1 after 90 minutes and still tied after half an hour's extra time, the players slogged it out until Hibs' Hugh Howie scored the golden goal in the 142nd minute – the longest single game ever to be played in Scotland. In the final, Hibs got off to a flyer, scoring in the first minute.

Aberdeen, though, were back on level terms before the interval. Despite Hibernian's goalkeeper Kerr pulling off a penalty save, it was the Dons who scored again. So the Scottish Cup – after eight years in wartime cold storage – finally left nearby Shawfield to make the long journey north to Pittodrie for the first time.

Hibs made the last four again in 1948 and their semi-final against Rangers attracted a UK record crowd for any club game outside a final. Willie Thornton scored the only goal of the game in front of 143,570 to take Rangers into their first final since 1936.

The match was a re-run of 1922 as Morton were their opponents. An early goal for the Greenock side threatened a similar outcome, too. Rangers equalised swiftly and although extra time was played (for the first time in a final other than a replay) there were no more goals.

But the appetites of the 129,176 in the crowd had scarcely been sated and the replay four days later produced an astonishing attendance of 133,570, creating a new midweek attendance record. Goals were again hard to come by and it wasn't until five minutes from the end of extra-time that Billy Williamson made the break-through with a header to bring the Scottish Cup back to Ibrox.

Rangers retained the trophy in 1949, easily beating Clyde 4-1 in the final with the aid of two penalties, and reached the final again in 1950, although Queen of the South took them to a replay in the last four. The only consolation for the Dumfries side was that the 58,975 attendance was the largest crowd ever to watch them in action.

East Fife barred Rangers' way in the final. But with only 30 seconds gone, Willie Findlay put Rangers ahead – the fastest goal in Scottish Cup Final history. Rangers settled the issue midway through the second half with two goals from Willie Thornton. They had equalled Queen's Park's achievement by winning the cup three years in succession for the second time.

Celtic marked their post-war re-emergence in the Scottish Cup Final of 1951. Opponents Motherwell, despite their League Cup success, seemed to freeze once again on the big day and a crowd in excess of 130,000 witnessed a disappointing game. John McPhail's 12th-minute strike was enough to bring the cup back to Parkhead for the first time in 14 years.

Motherwell at last made it all the way to the winner's rostrum the following year. An amazing aggregate of 238,224 had stumped up their cash for the three games they took to dispose of Hearts in the semi-final. The final against Dundee attracted 136,304 – the largest crowd ever to watch a Scottish club match not involving the Old Firm. Wilson Humphries won the cup for 'Well, laying on goals for Watson and Redpath before scoring himself. Centre-forward Kelly added a fourth.

In the 1953 final, John Prentice gave Rangers an early lead, only for Aberdeen to snatch an equaliser through Harry Yorston with 10 minutes remaining. The Dons were the better side in the replay but Billy Simpson snatched a goal for Rangers three minutes before the break and that was enough to take the Scottish Cup to Ibrox for the

WAITING FOR THE ACTION: Hampden in the 1950s.

14th time.

Such was the attraction of 1954's Scottish Cup semi-finals that both were played at Hampden – and the SFA was well rewarded, with more than 100,000 at both. Celtic and Motherwell drew their first match 2-2. Then, on April 10th, 1954, came one of the most remarkable humiliations either of the Old Firm has ever suffered. Almost 111,000 people gasped in disbelief as Aberdeen clinched a place in the final for the second successive season with an astonishing 6-0 thrashing of the Gers. It was a sad note on which 79-year-old Bill Struth ended 34 years as Rangers boss. Nine days previously he had announced his intention to retire at the end of the season.

Celtic's replay triumph over Motherwell set up an intriguing final. Another massive crowd of

HEART BEAT:
Willie Bauld hit
a treble against
Motherwell to
lift the League
Cup for Hearts
in 1955-56.

IN NEED OF A FACELIFT: The North Stand at Hampden shows its age in this photograph.

more than 130,000 saw Aberdeen recover from a shaky start to gradually take over as the first half progressed. But they couldn't find a way through a Celtic defence marshalled by Jock Stein. The deadlock was broken five minutes after the restart when a Neil Mochan shot was deflected into his own net by centre-half Young. Just 60 seconds later, Aberdeen equalised through Buckley. But just after the hour mark Willie Fernie provided the pass which allowed Irishman Sean Fallon to score the winner and give Celtic their first League and Cup "double" since 1914.

Celtic were back to defend their trophy in 1955. Waiting for them were Clyde and the TV cameras, who were there to screen the Scottish Cup Final live for the first time. Unfortunately for those on the terraces and those huddled in front of their tiny screens, the highlights were few and far between. Jimmy Walsh's goal seven minutes from half-time seemed to have secured the trophy for Celtic but, with two minutes to go, the Bully Wee's Archie Robertson swung in a corner which keeper Johnny Bonnar misjudged, helping the ball into the net.

The replay, without the cameras, was better but the only goal came from Clyde's Tommy Ring in 52 minutes to send the cup out Rutherglen way again. With the League Cup on display at Tynecastle and the title heading north to Pittodrie, Clyde's victory meant that for the second – and, so far, last – time, all three trophies resided elsewhere than Ibrox or Parkhead. Ominously, the published attendance for the replay – 68,735 – was the lowest for a Scottish Cup Final at Hampden since 1909.

Celtic gained revenge for their defeat by ousting Clyde at Hampden in the semi-finals a year later. Facing them in the final were Hearts who, incredibly,

HUNGARY FOR SUCCESS: The world's best team came to Hampden in 1954. The Hungarians had thrashed England 6-3 the previous year but they had a fight on their hands against Scotland. The stylish Magyars, however, eventually won 4-2.

were reaching this stage in the competition for the first time in 49 years. With just under 20 minutes played, Ian Crawford put the Edinburgh side ahead. There was some anxiety in their camp when John Cumming had to leave the field after a clash of heads with Willie Fernie. He re-emerged, head bandaged, for the second half. Within three minutes, Crawford had put Hearts two ahead.

Celtic pulled a goal back when Hearts' keeper Willie Duff was shoulder-charged into dropping the ball by Mike Haughney, who prodded it in to make the score 2-1. A perfectly legal goal in 1956 but a certain booking today. With ten minutes remaining Alfie Conn rifled in from 15 yards to seal a 3-1 win. The final whistle was the signal for a flaming torch to be lit on the terraces and for police to rugby-tackle ecstatic Hearts fans on the pitch.

Having ended Celtic's bid for a fourth successive final in the semis, Kilmarnock were favourites to defeat Falkirk and lift the trophy in 1957. But it was the Bairns who were the better side on the day and somewhat unlucky to have to return to Hampden after a 1-1 draw.

In the replay, the Bairns took a deserved lead but Killie equalised in the second half to send the game into extra-time. It was a mix-up in the Ayrshire defence which allowed Doug Moran to ram home the winner for Falkirk. Around 160,000 spectators had seen the two matches between a pair of Scotland's alleged underdogs.

The 1950s were a roller-coaster ride for Clyde. After winning the Cup in 1955, they were relegated in 1956, promoted in 1957 and back at Hampden for the Scottish Cup Final in 1958. They faced Hibernian, whose great days of the early fifties were in the past. For "Famous Five" legends such as Eddie Turnbull and Willie Ormond, this would be their last chance to win the Scottish Cup. It wasn't to be. A Johnny Coyle shot, which took a deflection off Hibs' back John Baxter, was enough to take the cup to Shawfield for the third time.

A knee injury to Andy Aitken had greatly hampered Hibs' efforts and in the 1959 final, Aberdeen were to be similarly undone by injury when full-back Dave Caldwell pulled a muscle. Although he returned to the pitch after five minutes, his fate was to play the traditional role of the injured cup final player. That is, to be stuck out on the left wing limping for the rest of the game.

Finals were often ruined as a spectacle by such injuries in the days before substitutions were allowed. St Mirren exploited the Dons' weakness, running out easy 3-1 winners. The Paisley side's victory ended something of a golden era for Scotland's provincial clubs at Hampden. For the fifth year in succession, neither of Glasgow's Big Two had got their hands on the cup. Indeed, for the first time since the days of Victorian gas lamps and hobnailed boots, neither had even reached the final for three successive years.

Even the crowd of 108,591 was significant. Never again would a Scottish Cup Final without an Old Firm presence attract a six-figure gate.

★ ★ ★ ★ ★

UP until the end of the Second World War, Hampden had staged just 17 full official internationals in more than 40 years – 15 of them against England, plus the visits from Austria and

Czechoslovakia. But the times they were a-changing and in the next 15 years, 40 games were played against not only our Home International neighbours Northern Ireland and Wales but also Belgium, France, Switzerland, Denmark, USA, Sweden, Norway, Hungary, Portugal, Yugoslavia, Spain, West Germany and Poland.

Crowds for these matches were immense. A friendly against France attracted 123,970 in 1949. Almost as many watched the Swiss, even though their visit came less than a fortnight after the Scots lost to England. Even the Americans enticed 107,765 fans along.

It was all part of the transition from regarding success in the games against England, Ireland and Wales as the ultimate international accolade. It began to be recognised that the rest of the world had not only caught up with the British Isles but had, in many cases, overtaken them at playing the world's most popular sport.

The biggest catalyst for this new outlook was the World Cup. Yet Scotland's introduction to the global contest was scarcely exotic. FIFA allowed the Home Internationals to act as a qualifying group for the 1950 tournament in Brazil and even permitted the first two in the group to qualify.

It was as close to an open invitation to Scotland and England as you could get. And 73,871 became witnesses to history on November 9th, 1949, when the first World Cup qualifying match was played at Hampden Park. Celtic's John McPhail and Alec Linwood of Clyde provided the goals in the 2-0 victory over Wales which appeared to guarantee Scotland's presence

TAKE THAT: The Hampden crowd roars its approval as Tommy Ring challenges the Swedish goalkeeper in the 1953 game.

in Rio. The SFA, however, decreed that Scotland would only go to the World Cup in Brazil if they were British champions. That meant they needed a draw against England at Hampden on April 15th, 1950, to share the title. All seemed well until Roy Bentley put England ahead shortly after the hour mark. Scotland threw everything into attack. A Willie Bauld effort smashed off the crossbar. There were claims it had crossed the line before being cleared but nothing was awarded. Scotland's six-match winning streak was at an end and, when the SFA decided to stick to their original decision, it was an end to their first-ever World Cup campaign, too. These days, it is impossible to imagine any country turning down the opportunity to play in the World Cup Finals.

But in 1950, that decision may well have been justified. The English team that left Hampden victorious returned from South America in shame, having been beaten by an unfancied USA team containing a handful of Scottish immigrants.

The SFA showed some forward thinking by inviting Hungary to Hampden for the final international of 1954. The Magyars had been the outstanding side in the world for years.

Despite losing the 1954 World Cup Final to West Germany, they were still acknowledged as THE team to beat. Talents such as Bozsik, Hidegkuti, Kocsis and the incomparable Ferenc Puskas were acclaimed the world over.

On a cold winter afternoon in mid-December 1954, a crowd of 113,056 turned up at Hampden to see this marvellous team in action. With less than a third of the match gone, Bozsik and Hidegkuti had fired them into a two-goal lead and the Scots looked to be heading for the kind of beating the Magyars had inflicted on England when they won 6-3 at Wembley in 1953.

Clyde's Tommy Ring pulled a goal back but

HAPPY BIRTHDAY: At the silver jubilee of Hampden Park in November 1953, schoolboy Max Murray, 17 – who would go on to play for Rangers – holds the original match ball with Jimmy McMenemy, Celtic, A F Currie, Queens Park, A Richmond, Queens Park, and Willie Loney, Celtic – who all played in the inaugural game – looking on.

Sandor made it 3-1 at half-time. When Hibs' Bobby Johnstone scored straight after the restart, the Hungarians knew they had a fight on their hands.

The difference in the way the game was played was demonstrated when Lawrie Reilly knocked out Hungarian keeper Farago with a shoulder charge. A fair challenge to the Scots: violent conduct to the Hungarians. With seconds remaining, Kocsis scored for Hungary to make the final score 4-2. It was defeat with honour for Scotland.

Many felt that this could be the first sign of a Scotland revival. It would prove to be a false dawn, even though Scotland were undefeated in their next nine Hampden outings. For the one traditional match which still held its allure in the post-war era was the match against England. And Scotland just could not register a home win over their oldest and greatest foes. In seven encounters between 1948 and 1960, the Scots lost five and drew twice.

They appeared to have laid the bogey to rest in 1956, leading 1-0 into the 90th minute, only for Johnny Haynes to equalise. There was a suggestion of handball but the goal stood and the emotions of 132,817 spectators transformed from ecstasy to agony in a matter of seconds.

At least it didn't count in terms of the World Cup. For the 1958 competition, Scotland were pitted against Spain

SHAKE ON IT:
George Young
exchanges gifts with
Yugoslavian captain
Stankovic at
Hampden Park
before an
international in
1956.

and Switzerland in the battle to qualify. The Spanish were as difficult an opponent as could be found. Real Madrid were easily the best club side in the world. From Barcelona came the magical inside-left Luis Suarez. As if that wasn't enough, under the lax rules operated by FIFA in those days, club football was allowed to determine nationality. Barcelona's gifted inside-right Ladislao Kubala, who was born in Budapest and had appeared internationally for both Hungary and Czechoslovakia, had become a naturalised Spaniard.

The most famous name in football at the time was that of Alfredo Di Stefano – still considered by many to be the greatest player of all time. The "Blond Arrow" had played for both his native Argentina and for Colombia. By 1956, FIFA had authorised his appearance for Spain.

True, the Scots had the South African-born John Hewie in their ranks but they set out to face this team of European champions and world superstars with a winger – Tommy Ring – who had just completed a season in the lower league in Scotland and who now had to switch his attentions from taking on defenders at Brechin to those from Barcelona. Jackie Mudie put Scotland ahead after 22 minutes but Kubala levelled eight minutes later. A Hewie penalty gave Scotland the half-time lead. Once again the Spanish hit back, with Suarez squaring the match five minutes into the second half. But with the roars of almost 90,000 voices bawling their encouragement from the Hampden slopes, Scotland pressed forward.

Mudie scored again with 20 minutes remaining, then capped a magnificent performance with his hat-trick goal to put the seal on one of Scotland's finest post-war triumphs.

The high from that game carried Scotland through the rest of the month. They won narrowly in Switzerland, then beat World Cup holders West Germany 3-1 in Stuttgart. The wounded Spaniards hit back at the end of the month, winning the return game 4-1 in the Bernabeu in Madrid. Fortunately for Scotland, Spain could only draw in Switzerland. A Hampden win against the Swiss would take Scotland to the World Cup Finals in Sweden.

Clyde's Archie Robertson put Scotland ahead but the Swiss came back to equalise. Mudie struck early in the second half and when Alex Scott of Rangers made it 3-1 after 70 minutes Scotland looked home and dry. But Switzerland hit back, scoring again to ensure a nervy last 10 minutes before the whistle blew to confirm Scotland's World Cup qualification.

The Scottish supporters in the crowd of 56,714 would have done well to pause and savour the moment. It would be 16 long years before they could experience anything like it again.

Scotland performed dismally in the 1958 Finals and by the time the 1960s approached were in need of fresh inspiration. As the new decade dawned, new heroes appeared. Men whose achievements are fondly remembered more than 40 years later.

An untried Scotland team recorded a fine 3-2 win over West Germany in front of more than 100,000 in May 1959. And there couldn't have been a better international debut for the inside-right from Falkirk than to score in the first minute. His name was John White.

There was a similar scoreline, but in the opposition's favour, when Scotland met Poland a year later. The inside-left who scored his first Hampden goal that day was a slim, fair-haired youth called Denis Law. In November 1960, as Scotland crushed Northern Ireland 5-2,

GOOD REPORT: The "crow's nest" Press Box at Hampden. left. It gave 102 newspaper reporters a fabulous view of the action.

CUP OF CHEER: Skipper Harry Haddock holds aloft the Scottish Cup as the Clyde team bus leaves Hampden after their triumph in 1958.

commentators noted the effective debut at left-half of a player Rangers had recently signed from Raith Rovers. Jim Baxter joined White and Law to form the last part of the glorious trio that would light up Hampden Park in the years ahead.

★ ★ ★ ★ ★

AWAY from the regular diet of cup finals and internationals, Hampden had many other memorable moments. The stadium turned airport in October 1947 for a helicopter display – a real novelty for the large crowd which watched the new fangled whirlybird hover, fly backwards and even "rescue" a "drowning sailor" from a tank of water.

Hockey was back at Hampden in 1958 after thirty years and this time it was the ladies of Scotland who took on and drew 2-2 with the touring South African ladies in March 1959, a thoroughly creditable performance by the Scots when set beside the thrashings bestowed that season by Wales, England and Ireland.

May 10th, 1947, was the date of a gala occasion. To mark the return of the home nations to FIFA, a match was arranged between a Great Britain side and The Rest of Europe. The Great Britain selection owed a lot to political considerations, comprising as it did of five Englishmen, three Scots, two Welsh and one from Northern Ireland: Swift (Manchester City, England), Hardwick (Middlesbrough, England), Hughes (Birmingham City, Wales), Macaulay (Brentford, Scotland), Vernon (West Bromwich Albion, Northern Ireland), Burgess (Tottenham Hotspur, Wales), Matthews (Blackpool, England), Mannion (Middlesbrough, England), Lawton (Chelsea, England), Steel (Morton, Scotland), Liddell (Liverpool, Scotland).

The Rest of Europe line-up was: Da Rui (France), Petersen (Denmark), Steffen (Switzerland), Carey (Eire), Parola (Italy), Ludl (Czechoslovakia), Lambrechts (Belgium), Gren (Sweden), Nordahl (Sweden), Wilkes (Netherlands), Prest (Denmark).

A remarkable 130,000 turned up to watch. They saw Wilf Mannion put the "home" team ahead in 22 minutes. Nordahl equalised and the game opened up into a fast, free-flowing contrast between the guile and intricate ball skills of the Europeans and the more direct, robust British game. As the British team were 4 goals up in 23 minutes the Hampden Roar was not heard that day as the crowd had expected a true contest. Both sides turned on a second-half exhibition and the final score was 6-1 to Britain. Amazingly enough when that game finished, thousands stayed behind to witness the final league game of the season for Third Lanark, who had switched the fixture to Hampden because of repair work being done at nearby Cathkin Park. Thirds lost 2-0 to Hibs.

★ ★ ★ ★ ★

IT wasn't just the seniors who drew huge crowds to Hampden, though. The Scottish Junior Cup Final of 1951 saw Petershill take on Irvine Meadow. Their clash attracted a crowd of 77,650 – a record for Junior football which will never be beaten. The only goal of the game came from Petershill's White, who only stayed long enough to collect his winner's medal before hurrying back to his RAF unit.

Football-hungry supporters were given the rare treat of summer football the same year. As part of the Festival of Britain, Glasgow Corporation funded a series of sporting events, with the main prize being the St Mungo Cup. Involving all six Glasgow clubs plus the top 10 league clubs from outside the city, the one-off trophy sparked huge interest. Celtic again proved to be adept at one-off competitions. In the Hampden final, they came back from two goals down to beat Aberdeen 3-2 in front of 80,264 – an incredible crowd for a Wednesday in August.

Two years later, there was an even more prestigious club competition. To mark the accession to the throne of the Queen Elizabeth, the Coronation Cup was contested by the elite of British football. Rangers, Celtic, Aberdeen and Hibernian represented Scotland while Arsenal, Manchester United, Newcastle United and Tottenham Hotspur were the English representatives.

All matches were played in Glasgow between May 11th and 20th, 1953. While Aberdeen were thrashed by Newcastle at Ibrox and Hibs took care of Spurs after a replay at Celtic Park, the Old Firm played their games at Hampden. Around 59,000 saw Celtic outplay newly-crowned English champions Arsenal, with a Bobby Collins

TIME FOR PRAYER: One of the biggest crowds Hampden has ever witnessed was in 1955 when legendary American evangelist Billy Graham came to preach as part of his "All Scotland Crusade".

CORONATION CRACKERS: The cream of British football came to Hampden in 1953 for the Coronation Cup. Rangers, Celtic, Aberdeen and Hibernian represented Scotland while Arsenal, Manchester United, Newcastle United and Tottenham Hotspur were the English teams taking part. Celtic lifted the silverware.

HEARING THE WORD: Another view of the huge crowd attracted to Hampden for Billy Graham's All Scotland Crusade.

goal direct from a corner kick taking them through. Two days later, Rangers lost 2-1 to Manchester United in front of 75,546. Then 73,000 saw Celtic beat Matt Busby's team 2-1.

As Hibs had easily swept aside Newcastle at Ibrox, it was an all-Scottish final on May 20th. Hibs were the favourites but Neilly Mochan shot Celtic ahead just before the half-hour mark. Celtic weathered a second-half storm, mainly thanks to the heroics of Johnny Bonnar in goal, and Jimmy Walsh made it 2-0 three minutes from time to seal an incredible victory in front of 117,060 spectators. Once again Celtic had demonstrated their flair for cup football.

On Coronation Day itself, June 2nd, 1953, the celebrations included an athletics programme at Hampden. British bantamweight boxing champion Peter Keenan fought an exhibition match with local featherweight John Kenny and, of course, there was football. Partick Thistle beat Third Lanark 2-0 in the final of a six-a-side tournament.

In October 1953, the ground celebrated its 50th birthday. But the occasion was marked only by a routine, if entertaining, league match which Queen's Park lost 4-2 against Ayr United. There were just 4,000 fans present but amongst them were the only four survivors of the 22 who had played in that first game half a century beforehand – A.F. Currie and Andy Richmond of Queen's and Jimmy McMenemy and Willie Loney from Celtic.

Hampden was the only feasible venue for American religious missionary Billy Graham's major outdoor evangelical meeting during his six week "All Scotland Crusade" in March and April 1955. Graham was a charismatic speaker drawing 100,000 worshippers to the ground and attracted more than two and a half million listeners during his visit.

April 30th, 1958, was a sad day as the curtain was brought down on Queen's Park's 42nd and final season in Division One. Only around 500 spectators were there to see them lose 2-1 to Kilmarnock. Although the Spiders still had an honourable role to play in Scottish football and would have their successes and promotions, they would never play in the top league again.

To some, it may have seemed the stadium the amateurs called home was also past its best. Yet although its capacity would steadily dwindle, Hampden still had many of its greatest days and nights ahead of it.

THE REAL DEAL: Hampden has witnessed many great games but few better than the European Cup Final between Real Madrid and Eintracht Frankfurt in 1960. Here Alfredo di Stefano scores for the Spaniards.

Chapter 6

From Success to Success in the Swinging Sixties

THEY were known as the Swinging Sixties, a time of innovation, daring and enormous social change. The accent was on youth but by the end of the decade, Hampden was a stadium of pensionable age. And it showed. It had been overtaken as the world's largest stadium by the Maracana in Brazil and outshone as Britain's best by a Wembley revamped for the 1966 World Cup. Hampden could only look on as better, more modern, if not always necessarily bigger stadia were built in Mexico and West Germany for both the Olympic Games and World Cup.

The days of heaving terraces were to end after tragedy struck at a football match elsewhere across the city and the impact on Hampden was immense and long-lasting. Yet the 1960s began with not only the greatest match in Hampden's history but also perhaps the most famous single game in the world – the 1960 European Cup Final between Real Madrid and Eintracht Frankfurt.

This one game took the blossoming tournament and made it flower into the greatest club competition in the world. Ever since those 90 minutes on the sunny evening of May 18th, 1960, football has been inspired by it. Real, winners of all four previous finals arrived in Scotland as favourites. The Germans, however, had trounced Rangers 12-4 on aggregate in the semi-finals and had their backers in the crowd of 129,621.

Real started slowly in the chill May air and Richard Kress nipped in behind their defence to score for the "Schlappekickers" in 18 minutes. Real were soon level when Canario's cross was converted by Alfredo di Stefano. They went ahead on the half hour mark when Egon Loy fumbled a cross and di Stefano reacted sharply to squeeze the ball home. Then Ferenc Puskas, the Hungarian "Galloping Major", slammed in a third from near the by-line and Real led 3-1 at the interval.

Puskas converted a penalty early in the second period and, with the Cup secured, the Spanish team relaxed and

EURO ZONE: The Real Madrid v Eintracht Frankfurt game in 1960 was Hampden's first big European night.
Above – Real keeper Dominguez misses a shot from Eintracht's Meier. Below – the match programme.

treated the crowd to an exhilarating football exhibition. Puskas added a fifth to complete his hat-trick midway through the half, then he headed another from a Gento cross.

The hard-working Erwin Stein left-footed home to make it 6-2 but straight from Puskas's kick-off, di Stefano ran fully 40 yards to smack the ball past Loy for HIS hat-trick. Stein pulled back another and Real still had time to hit the post before referee Jack Mowat, the only Scot on the field, blew his final whistle on a 7-3 Madrid win.

The spectators roared their appreciation realising they had just witnessed something a little bit special and, as the Real players trotted round Hampden with the trophy, thousands of small boys and not-so-small boys rushed out into streets, parks and gardens all over Britain to practice the new skills they'd just thrilled to on their televisions.

HAMPDEN had lagged behind other grounds in floodlighting. With the advent of midweek European competition and the increasing number of

120

World Cup qualifiers and friendlies, awkward kick-off times such as 4pm or 6.15pm were badly affecting crowds. At last, action was taken and on October 18th, 1961, the Hampden floodlights were officially opened with a challenge match between Rangers and Eintracht Frankfurt, which the Germans won 3-2 in front of a massive 104,679.

A real glamour fixture was next on the agenda on November 1st, 1961, when the Scottish League met their Italian counterparts for the first time. What a star-studded line-up it was. Apart from established Italian stars, they included the top foreign players in Italy, including Kurt Hamrin, the Swedish winger, the Welsh "gentle giant" John Charles, Gerry Hitchens from England and, of course, Scotland's own Denis Law, of Torino. A crowd of 67,000 saw a 1-1 draw, with Ralph Brand scoring for the Scots and Hitchens netting for the Italian League. Bob Crampsey, in his centenary history of the Scottish League, says it was "perhaps the best result the Scottish League ever achieved".

UEFA were so delighted with the SFA's handling of the 1960 European Cup Final that they awarded the 1962 Cup-Winners' Cup Final to Hampden. On paper, it seemed an attractive contest. Atletico Madrid against Fiorentina, who were defending the trophy they had won by beating Rangers in the first final the year before. But only 27,389 could be persuaded to attend the match, which ended in a 1-1 draw. No provision had been made for a replay, so both teams had to go to Stuttgart four months later, when Atletico triumphed 3-0.

Undaunted, the SFA were again happy to stage the 1966 European Cup Winners' Cup Final at Hampden. The

BACK IN BUSINESS: 1963 saw the first Old Firm Scottish Cup Final for 35 years. In this picture Celtic's Duncan McKay (wearing No.2 on his shorts) heads over the bar as Rangers forward Jimmy Millar closes in.

ideal finalists would have been Celtic and Liverpool, managed by the Scottish legend Bill Shankly. But these teams clashed in the last four, where Liverpool emerged, somewhat luckily, victorious.

In the final they faced Borussia Dortmund, who had beaten holders West Ham United in the other semi-final. Liverpool did most of the attacking but the West German team – with Hans Tilkowski, their national team regular, in goal – were hard nuts to crack. It was Dortmund who took the lead through Sigi Held in 62 minutes. Six minutes later, Roger Hunt equalised and the match went into extra time. Four minutes into the second period, right-winger Reinhard Libuda won the cup for the Germans.

The presence of Shankly's team had ensured the crowd was of a more respectable size – 41,657 – but it was still far fewer than had been hoped for. It would be several years before the SFA again bid for a European final.

★ ★ ★ ★ ★

ON the club front, Rangers began the decade as they meant to go on, beating Kilmarnock 2-0 in the 1960 Scottish Cup Final despite starting the match as underdogs. By the end of the Sixties, however, one man had taken a stranglehold on Scottish football – Jock Stein.

Hampden had figured prominently in his earlier playing success with Celtic, who he captained to success in the 1953 Coronation Cup Final and 1954 Scottish Cup Final. Yet while his achievements with the Parkhead club are rightly honoured, it is sometimes forgotten that Stein's first major managerial success was with Dunfermline

Athletic. He led the unfashionable Fife team to their first Scottish Cup Final in 1961 and they belied the old adage about only being allowed one crack at the Old Firm when they beat Celtic 2-0 in a replay.

Rangers then embarked on a three-year winning streak achieved by what many Ibrox fans consider to be their greatest-ever side. They brushed aside St Mirren in the 1962 final with goals from Ralph Brand and Davy Wilson. A spirited Celtic side surprisingly forced a replay in 1963 in the first Old Firm final for 35 years but the same lethal strike duo of Brand (2) and Wilson earned Rangers a thumping 3-0 victory.

The 1964 final between Rangers and Dundee was an entertaining game between two well-matched teams. Surprisingly, it was still goalless after more than 70 minutes, when Jimmy Millar gave Rangers the lead. Almost immediately Kenny Cameron equalised. With under two minutes left, a replay beckoned. Then a Willie Henderson cross was headed in by Millar. Almost from the restart, Brand pounced to make the final score a lopsided 3-1. History was made. For the third time, Rangers had won three in a row.

Jock Stein was back at Hampden in 1965 but this time Dunfermline were the opposition as he guided Celtic to the first of many trophies under his leadership. The Pars led twice but a memorable late header from Billy McNeill took the Scottish Cup to Parkhead for the first time since Stein himself held the cup aloft in 1954.

Between 1909-1963 there had been just one Old Firm Final. Now they appeared with monotonous regularity. There was little in their first, goalless 1966 encounter to provide any lasting memory for the massive crowd present. The replay was a better game, with Celtic well on top. It also looked like finishing scoreless until a Kai Johansen

THE MAX FACTOR: The 1962 Scottish Cup semi-final between Rangers and Motherwell attracted another huge crowd. Here, Max Murray of Rangers scores past Well keeper Alan Wylie.

piledriver secured the cup for Rangers and gave Scot Symon his last trophy as Rangers manager.

Celtic were back again in 1967 and they overcame a stuffy Aberdeen side 2-0 with both goals coming from Willie Wallace. It is worth noting the Celtic line-up that day: Ronnie Simpson, Jim Craig, Tommy Gemmell, Bobby Murdoch, Billy McNeill (captain), John Clark, Jimmy Johnstone, Willie Wallace, Steve Chalmers, Bertie Auld, Bobby Lennox. That was the same 11 who, less than a month later, became the first British team to win the European Cup and who have gone down in history as the Lisbon Lions.

Their European triumph led to Hampden hosting Celtic's World Club Championship first-leg match against Argentina's Racing Club, the champions of South America. Among the crowd of 103,000 was Prime Minister Harold Wilson. Sadly, the match itself failed dismally to live up to its billing. Celtic were faced with tactics they had never before encountered as the Argentinian players resorted to spitting, gouging and even punching. A Billy McNeill header 20 minutes from time gave Celtic a 1-0 victory on the night. It wasn't enough. They lost the return 2-1 and then, amid scenes of mayhem, were beaten in a Montevideo play-off as Celtic finally retaliated in kind, only to see four players sent off. What should have been a celebration of football descended into onfield barbarism.

The battered and bruised Celts were fairly and squarely put out of 1968's Scottish Cup in the early rounds by Dunfermline as the Fife side marched to their third final in seven years. Opponents Hearts had knocked out Rangers, but the attendance for the final – 56,365 – was the smallest crowd since the First World War. Most of the action was compressed into a 20-minute spell midway through the second half when all the goals were scored, leaving Dunfermline victorious by 3-1.

The 1969 Scottish Cup Final confirmed the gulf in class between Celtic and Rangers as a catalogue of errors led to an overwhelming 4-0 triumph for the Parkhead side. And while the green half of Glasgow celebrated, Hampden looked a strange sight in the second half, with one end of the ground half-empty as thousands of disconsolate Rangers supporters made their way home long before the end. This game has also been credited with destroying the Ibrox career of Alex Ferguson, who was posted missing in action after two minutes as an unmarked Billy McNeill scored with a free header.

It was Celtic's turn to leave Hampden empty-handed in 1970. In a repeat of 1967, they faced Aberdeen in the final with one eye on the European Cup. The Dons took the lead through a controversial Joe Harper penalty. Twice Celtic appealed for a penalty themselves and twice referee Bobby Davidson turned them down. He also ruled out a Lennox strike before the game finished sensationally.

Derek McKay had appeared from nowhere to score the winners in the previous two rounds. With eight minutes to play, he beat Tommy Gemmell to the ball and scored to put the Dons two up. Lennox pulled one back with two minutes remaining but, as Celtic piled forward in search of an equaliser, McKay broke away to score his second and Aberdeen's third to take the cup north.

Manager Eddie Turnbull at last got his hands on the trophy denied to him as a player. Martin Buchan, at 21, became the youngest cup-winning captain. But the glory belonged to McKay – a player unheard of before the quarter-finals and who faded back into obscurity afterwards just as quickly as he had risen.

FOUR days after losing to Aberdeen, Celtic returned to Hampden to face Leeds United in the

CHANGING TIMES: Managers Jock Stein, of Celtic, and Juan Pizutti, of Racing Club, inspect the Hampden dressing room before the infamous World Club Championship match in 1967.

BATTLE OF BRITAIN: Hampden Park was the only football ground in Scotland big enough to hold the Celtic v Leeds United European Cup Semi Final in 1970.

semi-final of the European Cup. The Parkhead side had won the first leg 1-0 at Elland Road and played the return at Hampden, as Celtic Park could not possibly hold all the people who wanted to see this tie.

Forget the paler imitations down the years which have been labelled "Battle of Britain". This was the real thing. The respective champions of Scotland and England, both at the peak of their powers. There were 136,505 people inside Hampden as the game kicked off. This was more than had attended the 1960 Final and was a record for any European competition. It is one which is likely to stand for all time.

Most of that vast horde were silenced in 14 minutes when Leeds' captain Billy Bremner blasted a 25-yarder past Celtic keeper Evan Williams into the top corner of the net to level the tie on aggregate. Celtic soon responded and seized control of the game. Two minutes after the restart, John Hughes beat Jack Charlton to an Auld cross to head home the equaliser. Five minutes later, Wee Jinky Jimmy Johnstone stroked a pass into the path of Bobby Murdoch, who hit a fierce shot past David Harvey in the Leeds goal. A double victory over England's best.

The bulk of the vast crowd stayed behind to cheer their heroes as they embarked on a triumphal lap of honour round Hampden. There were few then who would have bet against them winning a second European Cup. But they didn't. Celts lost their way in Milan's San Siro and, even though the game went to extra-time, they were beaten by Feyenoord.

★ ★ ★ ★ ★

UNTIL then the province of the underdog, the League Cup became the plaything of the Old Firm during the 1960s

SHAKE ON IT: Skippers Billy McNeill, of Celtic, and Billy Bremner, of Leeds United, shake hands before the European Cup clash at Hampden.

as the Glasgow giants realised the value of winning the first trophy of the season. A League Cup victory also guaranteed a place in Europe – a fast-growing and lucrative venture for the Big Two.

Rangers began the trend by defeating the two main challengers to their supremacy – Kilmarnock and Hearts – in the first finals of the decade. Then, in the one season when the Glaswegian grip was broken, Hearts and Killie faced each other in the final in October 1962.

It was a strange affair, played out on the weekend that the Cuban missile crisis reached its peak, with humanity on the brink of Armageddon. Yet more than 50,000 turned up to see Hearts win 1-0 after referee Tom "Tiny" Wharton ruled out a late "equaliser" from the Ayrshire team for a handball that was spotted by no one else in the stadium.

The "wee" teams still had some say in this competition. In 1963-64, Berwick Rangers reached the semi-finals before losing to their Glasgow counterparts 3-1 before a poor crowd of just over 16,000.

It was a different story when another Second Division side faced Rangers in the final. For Morton had taken Scottish football by storm. They smashed all sorts of records in Division Two and took the top league scalps of Motherwell and Hibs on the road to Hampden. Such was the interest generated by the Greenock side that the League Cup Final gate topped 100,000 for the first time.

Unfortunately for the Cappielow

team, the occasion proved too much for them and Rangers ran out easy winners by 5-0. It was a personal triumph for striker Jim Forrest, who scored a record-breaking four goals.

It was Forrest who struck again the next year, scoring twice as Rangers beat Celtic 2-1. This was the last final appearance as a manager for Jimmy McGrory, more than a quarter of a century after he led Kilmarnock to the 1938 Scottish Cup Final.

The Ayrshire club featured in a sensational contest in the last four in 1965-66. Kilmarnock were reigning league champions but their much-vaunted defence was torn to ribbons as Rangers beat them 6-4. It was hard on Killie winger Tommy McLean, who had scored a hat-trick.

Celtic, under new boss Jock Stein, gained revenge for their previous defeat as two penalties from John Hughes gave them a 2-1 win over Rangers in front of a record attendance for the League Cup Final of 107,609. It was the start of a remarkable run in the tournament for Celtic, who reached the final in every one of Stein's 13 seasons in charge. Added to McGrory's last outing, it gave them 14 successive League Cup Final appearances at Hampden.

In 1966-67, Celtic's all-conquering season, the League Cup was the first trophy bagged when a Bobby Lennox goal was enough to see off Rangers in yet another Old Firm final. But if

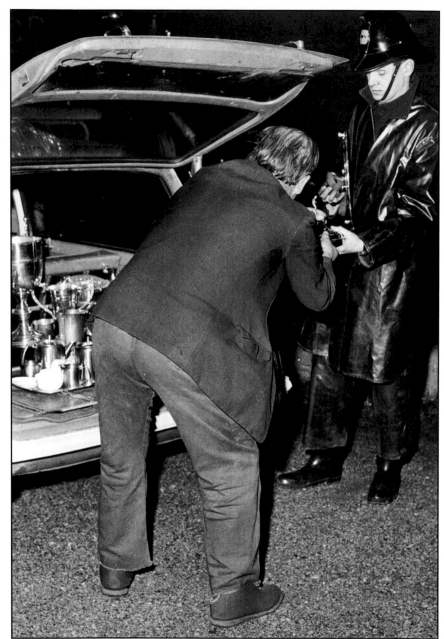

ARSON ATTACK: Firemen help officials load trophies into a car to save them from the blaze, left. The clock above the entrance stopped at 11.32, right.

thrills were scarce in that final, they were in plentiful supply during the next two seasons as the goals flooded in. First came a battle with Dundee, which swung first one way, then the other, before Celtic clinched victory 5-3. Then came a demolition of Hibernian as Celtic, aided by a Lennox hat-trick, crushed the Edinburgh team 6-2.

Unusually, that 1968-69 final was actually played in April 1969, rather than the winter of 1968. The blame for this lay with an arsonist who set fire to Hampden's South Stand on the night of October 21st, 1968. The blaze gutted much of the centre stand, destroying the main administration offices, the visitors' dressing room and 1,000 seats.

Queen's Park committee member Junior Omand and club coach Harry Davis dashed in at one stage to rescue the Centenary Cup. The clock above the entrance bore silent witness, its hands stopping at 11.32. The League Cup Final due the following Saturday had to be postponed. The suspicion that all was not innocent gained credence when Ibrox Stadium suffered a similar fire the following night, then Cathkin's dilapidated stand went up in November.

Another small fire at Hampden in April caused minimal damage but the police were absolutely certain there was an fire-raiser at work when Ibrox lost another 250 seats in May 1969. A local man was arrested when police and the fire brigade raced to Hampden yet again on the last day of June 1969 to deal with yet another outbreak. This time, the fire was caught early but more than 200 seats were destroyed.

The damage did not stop the 1969-70 League Cup Final returning to its more usual late autumn date. Celtic's

HAMPDEN IN FLAMES: Firemen battle to save the stand during the blaze of October 21, 1968.

opponents were St Johnstone, who put up a spirited fight. But an early goal from Bertie Auld was enough to give Celts a record fifth successive triumph.

Their bid to make it six in a row was almost halted in the semi-final by Second Division Dumbarton, who held Celtic to a 0-0 draw, then gave them a real scare in the replay before losing 4-3. For all that, few expected Celtic to lose to Rangers in the 1970-71 Final. Fewer still would have dared predict that a 16-year-old would determine the outcome. But that was precisely what happened as Ibrox boss Willie Waddell threw teenage striker Derek Johnstone into the fray.

In only his second start for the club, the youngster outjumped both Billy McNeill and Jim Craig to head home the game's only goal in 41 minutes. Rangers' victory was also the first major trophy for Waddell as their manager and the club's first in over four years. It was witnessed by the last six-figure crowd to watch a League Cup Final.

★ ★ ★ ★ ★

THE early 1960s was a great time to be a Scotland fan. In 13 Hampden internationals between November 1960 and November 1964, Scotland won 12 and lost just once. Yet this success came after one of the worst Scottish humiliations ever when they lost 9-3 at Wembley in 1961. Just a few months later, they faced a talented Czechoslovakia team in a World Cup qualifier and twice came from behind to beat them 3-2 thanks to a late Denis Law goal. That took the Scots into a play-off in Brussels, where they lost in extra-time to the Czechs who went on to reach the 1962 World Cup Final in Chile.

In April 1962, Scotland proved their revival was substantial. Davy Wilson gave them an early lead against England but despite dominating the game Scotland had nothing more to show for their efforts with just two minutes left on the clock.

In the past, this would have been around the time for

HAMPDEN HERO: Denis Law was always a great favourite with the Hampden fans. In 1962, he scored four goals in a 5-1 win against Northern Ireland.

England to score. But not this time. Scotland were awarded a penalty which Eric Caldow calmly put away to seal a memorable victory – Scotland's first "official" Hampden success over England since 1937. How the crowd roared as the players saluted them on an emotional lap of honour at the end of the game.

Next opponents Uruguay upset things with a 3-2 win but Scotland returned to their rampant best, beating Northern Ireland 5-1, with Law scoring four to equal Billy Steel's record.

The Law Man also hit two against Austria in an infamous match which was abandoned by English referee Jim Finney. With 11 minutes to play and Scotland leading 4-1, the Austrians had resorted to onfield brawling.

Just how good this Scotland team was is a matter for endless debate. They lost in unlikely places such as Norway and Ireland but also won at Wembley and destroyed Spain 6-2 in Madrid. But, as the SFA declined to enter Scotland for the Nations Cup (now the European Championship), we shall never know for certain. What we do know is that Spain won the European title in 1964 and no Scot needs to be reminded of what England did in 1966.

Neither of these two countries were a match for the Scotland of Law, Baxter, White, Mackay and co. And what a player Law was. Exactly one year to the day after scoring four at Hampden against Northern Ireland, he repeated the trick in a 6-1 win over Norway on November 1963. Little wonder that in 1964 Law became the only Scot to receive the prestigious European Footballer of the Year award.

Sharing the limelight that year was Alan Gilzean. It was the Dundee player who broke the deadlock with less than 20 minutes to go when he scored the only goal of the game against England in April 1964.

As they left Hampden that day no one in the crowd of 133,245 could have had any idea that they had seen one of

Scotland's all-time greats perform at the stadium for the very last time. John White – nicknamed "The Ghost" on account of his ability to appear in a danger position seemingly from nowhere and master of the raking, defence-splitting pass – was killed when he was struck by lightning on a golf course in July of that year. The Tottenham Hotspur star was just 27 years old.

The team had to pick themselves up from the tragedy and concentrate on qualifying for the World Cup Finals in England. They got off to a good start but the crunch came in the home match against Poland. There were 107,580 at Hampden that October evening – a new record for a UK floodlit match.

Skipper Billy McNeill gave Scotland the lead after 14 minutes and, though it was an edgy match, his goal looked to have won the tie. But with only six minutes remaining, the roof fell in on Scotland as they conceded two late goals to allow the Poles to become the first continental team to win a World Cup match at Hampden Park.

As a consequence of this defeat Scotland were left with the daunting task of beating Italy twice to book their passage south of the border. On a night of high Hampden passion, Jim Baxter was awarded the captaincy for the first time. But the Italians, the masters of catenaccio – massed defence – seemed unperturbed by wave after wave of Scottish attacks. They looked to have secured the draw that was their aim when John Greig burst through with two minutes left and sent 100,000 Scottish supporters home deliriously happy as he smashed home the winner.

But an injury-ravaged side went down to defeat in Naples in a game which condemned the Scots to watch the World Cup Finals on TV. From being virtually unbeatable, Scotland became the team that couldn't win a game in 1966. They lost 4-3 in a thrilling match with England before they were humiliated at home, losing 3-0 to Holland. The

GLORY, GLORY: Hampden during a Queen's Park match.

Dutch weren't ranked in those days, as the attendance of just 16,513 showed, yet their Hampden victory was the first sign that a new power was arising in world football.

The unexpected Dutch triumph had one lasting effect on the Scottish game. For decades, debate had raged fiercely over the inclusion of Anglos, as those who plied their trade south of the border were described.

In these days, when grandmothers' birth certificates are eagerly scanned in order to discern the slightest Scottish connection, it seems a strange argument to say the least. However, the 11 players beaten by Holland all played for Scottish League clubs. It was the last time Scotland would take the field with an "all-tartan" team.

Next up at Hampden were Portugal, whose star player was the supremely talented Eusebio. But fewer than 25,000 saw Jose Torres score the only goal of the game deep into the second half. For the first time, Scotland had lost three international matches in succession at Hampden.

The one name in international football guaranteed to awaken the slumbering supporters was that of Brazil. The defending world champions enticed almost 75,000 to Hampden. They weren't there just to honour the team that had won the last two World Cups.

Nor were they there simply to see the stars of the future, such as the young Gerson and Jairzinho. They were there to see one player only – Edson Arantes do Nascimento. Or, to give him the name by which he is better known, Pele.

Scotland got off to a dream start, with Stevie Chalmers scoring after just 38 seconds. And even though Servilio equalised, this was a much better performance from the Scots. The fans left content with a 1-1 draw and with memories of seeing the world's greatest player in action.

UEFA acted as kindly as FIFA had once done by allowing the Home Internationals for 1966-67 and '67-68 to serve as a qualifying group for the 1968 Nations Cup. But the great side of the early 1960s had broken

BRAWL GAME: Denis Law scores in the 1963 match between Scotland and Austria at Hampden. It was abandoned when the visitors, losing 4-1, started fighting on the field.

up. White was dead. Law's appearances were restricted by injury. Time and injury had taken their toll on Dave Mackay.

In November 1967, as Scotland scraped past Wales 3-2, another of the greats departed the scene. No one knew it at the time, but as the players trooped off the field it was the last time Jim Baxter would do so in a Scotland jersey. Aged just 28, this was the midfield maestro's 34th and final international appearance. Baxter had performed one last great service for his country with his outstanding performance in the 3-2 victory at Wembley in 1967. But all the good work of that day was undone by losing in Northern Ireland.

In order to comply with UEFA's timetable for the European Championship, the England game at Hampden was brought forward to February 1968. At stake was a quarter-final tie with Spain. And, thanks to that defeat in Belfast, Scotland needed to win.

Scotland started brightly, with Charlie Cooke creating havoc down the right flank. And it seemed they had gone ahead in the 18th minute when Bobby Lennox poked the ball into the net after keeper Gordon Banks had dropped it. But the referee spotted a foul undetected by 129,474 spectators and chalked it off. Two minutes later, disaster struck when Martin Peters shot home from 20 yards to put England ahead. John Hughes equalised but after the break England put the shackles on Cooke, while the two Bobbys – Charlton and Moore – took control of the match. Long before the end it was clear that England would leave with the draw they had come for.

As one competition finished, another got under way. Scotland's next Hampden game was their first qualifier for the 1970 World Cup in Mexico. Austria, in their first appearance at Hampden since the infamous match of 1963, stunned the Scots by taking an early lead. But the familiar figure of Denis Law and the tigerish Billy Bremner snatched the goals which brought Scotland victory.

West Germany, runners-up in 1966, were the seeded team in Scotland's group and they showed why in front of nearly 100,000 at Hampden in April 1969, when a striker fast making a name for himself – Gerd Muller – put them ahead near the end of the first half.

This was a team of rare quality. Alongside Muller was Helmut Haller, who had scored in the 1966 World Cup Final. Held and Overath were world class, too. And at the back were the awesome Franz Beckenbauer and Karl-Heinz Schnellinger, aided by a lively little full-back called Hans-Hubert Vogts.

But Scotland kept plugging away and, with two minutes left, Charlie

GIRL POWER: The Ayr Majorettes entertain the big Hampden crowd before the 1966 Scotland v England international.

BRAZIL-IANT: Of all the big names who have graced Hampden none comes bigger than Brazilian superstar Pele.

Cooke produced a sublime piece of skill to fool the defence as he threaded the ball through to Bobby Murdoch, who equalised. At 1-1 it was honours even and all still to play for.

Group minnows Cyprus were next to visit Hampden. Aware that goal difference could decide the group, manager Bobby Brown demanded a big victory… and he got it. Colin Stein helped himself to four goals as the Scots romped to an 8-0 win. All to no avail. Four days later, the Germans blasted TWELVE past the Cypriots. Then, in a terrific game in Hamburg, Scotland were narrowly beaten 3-2. For the third successive time, they had failed to reach the World Cup Finals.

That failure meant 1970 was a flat year internationally, summed up by a 0-0 draw with England at Hampden –

the first scoreless game since the inaugural match between the countries also finished 0-0 back in 1872.

The Scottish football public were given a treat in May 1970 when the country hosted UEFA's Under-18 Championship, with the final set for Hampden. Stars of the future on display included Alain Giresse of France, the Dutch quartet of Neeskens, Rep and the Van Der Kerkhof twins, Leighton James of Wales and two outstanding West Germans – Paul Breitner and a youngster called Rainer Bonhof.

The home side did well to finish in third place and no fewer than seven of the squad of 16 – John Brownlie, Alfie Conn, Arthur Graham, Ian Munro, Derek Parlane, Alan Rough and Graeme Souness – went on to play full international football.

A talented Dutch side faced East Germany in the final and, with the teams still tied 1-1 after extra time, the Germans called correctly on the toss of a coin. It was an unsatisfactory end to an enthralling tournament.

★ ★ ★ ★ ★

SPEEDWAY had been part of Glasgow's sporting scene since the 1920s but when the new M8 motorway drove right through the White City stadium in the late 1960s, Hampden became the sport's unlikely new home when the famous Glasgow Tigers relocated there in April 1969.

Lord Provost John Johnston cut the tapes on the new era. Club captain Jim McMillan, Norwegian Oyvind Berg and fans favourite Charlie Monk led Tigers to eighth place in the British League. Bolstered by a great Hampden record – they dropped only one league point at home – Tigers again finished eighth in 1970.

But Tigers couldn't maintain their progress and finished near the foot of the table in the

SAFE HANDS: England keeper Gordon Banks thwarts Scotland in the 1966 international at Hampden, which the visitors won 4-3.

ON YER BIKE: Hampden was the home of Glasgow Tigers speedway team in 1969 and many a thrilling race was held at the ground before they relocated to Coatbridge.

following two seasons. Towards the end of 1972 tragedy struck with the on-track death of Norwegian Svein Kaasa and an inevitably sombre season petered out.

The sport had run its course at the National Stadium as escalating running costs, dwindling crowds and the council's refusal to allow music on race nights all contributed to a lack of atmosphere. It was a sad end as Tigers departed for Albion Rovers' Cliftonhill ground in Coatbridge.

By then, tragic events elsewhere had already sparked off serious debate about the future of Hampden Park.

It was no longer a question of how many fans could be squeezed into a stadium, it was rightly considered even more important that they should also be able to leave it in safety. The design of football grounds had become a matter of life and death.

TIGER, TIGER: The Glasgow speedway team's line-up in 1969, from left – Mike Hiftle, Oyvind Berg, Charlie 'Maximum' Monk, Bobby Beaton, Willie Templeton, Jimmy McMillan (captain) and Russ Dent.

WASHING DAY: Queen's Park shirts dry in the breeze outside Hampden, left. Not a sight you will see in these modern times.

DOG DAY: An alsatian guards the Hampden terraces. Well, we've all heard of a crowd of one man and his dog...

THREE GIANTS OF THE GAME: Legendary referee Tom "Tiny" Wharton checks out the result of the coin toss with Old Firm captains John Greig and Billy McNeill before the 1971 Scottish Cup Final. In the background, Hampden's North Stand and Terracing is jam-packed.

Chapter 7

Years of Tragedy and Triumph

SOCIETY had changed at breakneck speed throughout the 1960s, yet Hampden had remained serenely aloof from the clamour for change. Apart from new floodlights and a roof which had been erected over the West terracing in 1968, the ground had witnessed only minor upgrading.

Massive crowds had continued to flock to its slopes to sway and cheer amid a crush which usually provoked more amusement than alarm. And the final whistle had always been the signal for a stampede down the steep exit stairways in order to catch a bus or train towards home or a friendly hostelry.

But the reckless jamming together of frail human bodies lost any charm or innocence it had ever possessed on Saturday, January 2nd, 1971, when 66 people were crushed to death on Stairway 13 at Ibrox Park. It was the worst disaster in Scottish football history. Devastation and loss felt across Scotland and beyond cannot be overstated. The legacy of the tragedy still haunts many to this day.

The most immediate – and long-lasting – effect of the disaster was to focus attention on the state of football grounds and, in particular, spectator safety. It was the beginning of the end of the days of massed terraces, the entrance of long-reluctant authorities to take up safety issues and legislate for improvements and the start of the move towards all-seater stadia.

The priority was to provide assistance for the families of the bereaved. A benefit match between a Scotland XI and a Rangers-Celtic select was swiftly arranged for January 27th at Hampden. The Scotland team was a full-strength side, while the Old Firm team consisted of five from Rangers and three Celts plus three guest stars. Peter Bonetti of Chelsea kept goal and the Manchester United superstars Bobby Charlton and George Best completed the line-up. The Scots won 2-1 with goals from Archie Gemmill and Peter Lorimer. Best scored for the Old Firm. More

FORSYTH SAGA: The winner in the Centenary Scottish Cup Final in 1973 was scored by Tom Forsyth, with a miskick from six inches to clinch a 3-2 win for Rangers over Celtic. It was the last time a crowd of more than 100,000 saw a match at Hampden.

importantly, 81,405 turned up and paid over £50,000 at the gate. While no amount of money could possibly compensate for the loss of life, it was tangible evidence of the depth of sympathy felt right across Scotland.

★ ★ ★ ★ ★

SUPERFICIALLY, the Ibrox Disaster appeared to have altered nothing, as the 1971 Scottish Cup Final and replay were both attended by more than 100,000 spectators, with Celtic beating Rangers 2-1 after a 1-1 draw. But, behind the scenes, changes were afoot that would radically alter the face of the game in Scotland. Throughout the 1970s, new laws came into force compelling sports grounds to obtain licences from local authorities, and police recommendations on crowd limits and segregation measures came into effect.

Another massive crowd saw the most one-sided final of the 20th century as Celtic, inspired by hat-trick hero John "Dixie" Deans crushed Hibs 6-1. Old Firm finals – once a rarity – now came along as routine. 1973's clash was the fifth inside a decade. Fortunately, in the tournament's centenary year, the teams served up a classic. Derek Parlane and Alfie Conn had put Gers ahead after Kenny Dalglish's opener but George Connelly converted a penalty to leave the side's at stalemate until Tom Forsyth turned unlikely hero for the Ibrox side.

With an hour gone, the defender scrambled home the winner from a few inches. Another royal visitor to Hampden, Princess Alexandra, presented the trophy to John Greig, sparking off wild celebrations in the Light Blue half of the 122,714 crowd – the last time a six-figure crowd attended a football match in Scotland.

Celtic picked themselves up to win the next two finals against unfancied Dundee United and Airdrie. The latter game, in 1975, marked the end of the remarkable playing career of Billy McNeill. After 18 years, 29 caps, 23 winners' medals including the

European Cup, Caesar bowed out in style, holding the Scottish Cup aloft for the seventh time before being lifted by his teammates to receive the acclaim of the Hampden crowd.

The 1976 final is remembered for Derek Johnstone's goal against Hearts after just 42 seconds setting up a 3-1 win for Rangers that clinched their first domestic treble since 1964. A controversial Andy Lynch penalty gave Celtic victory in another Old Firm showdown in 1977 before Gers came back in 1978 to defeat Aberdeen and secure yet another treble in John Greig's final match. The Ibrox legend retired from playing with 44 caps and 16 winners' medals. Like his great rival McNeill, his last act as a player was to climb up the hallowed South Stand steps to receive the Scottish Cup.

The 1979 competition illustrated that the domestic game was struggling. Fewer than 10,000 fans made the long trek to Hampden to see two of the country's top teams – Hibs and Aberdeen – in the semi-finals. The Edinburgh side made it through to face Rangers but the sides played out two dull goal-less draws before the second replay sparked into life. Sadly, it was too late for most of the fans. The crowd was just over 30,000 – the lowest ever for a Scottish Cup Final at Hampden.

After 226 minutes of goal-less toil, Tony Higgins gave Hibs the lead. A double from Derek Johnstone put Gers in front but Ally McLeod's penalty took the tie to extra time. There were just 10 minutes left when veteran Hibee Arthur Duncan headed past his own keeper to give Rangers the cup.

★ ★ ★ ★ ★

ALTHOUGH the Scottish Cup appeared to have lost its capacity to shock, the League Cup certainly had not. Partick Thistle reached their fourth League Cup Final in 1971-72 but few held out much hope for success against Celtic. Certainly none could have expected they were about to witness the finest hour-and-a-half in the

CROSSING THE GREAT DIVIDE: Celtic forward Alfie Conn is tackled by Rangers defender Kenny Watson in the 1977 Scottish Cup Final, which the Parkhead club won 1-0. Four years earlier, Conn had scored for Rangers in their 3-2 cup triumph.

SHOCK OF THE CENTURY: Partick skipper Alex Rae and Celtic's captain for the day Bobby Murdoch lead their teams out of the tunnel at Hampden before the 1971 League Cup Final. The scoreline sent shockwaves round the football world – Thistle won 4-1.

Maryhill club's history. Goals from Alex Rae and Bobby Lawrie inside 15 minutes gave Thistle a dream start. Two more strikes from Dennis McQuade and Jimmy Bone made the half-time score 4-0. Celts kept up a non-stop barrage in the second half but had just one goal – from a promising youngster called Kenny Dalglish – to show for their efforts. It was one of the biggest shocks in Scottish football history.

That victory opened the door for others. Hibs beat Celtic 2-1 in the 1972-73 final and the Hoops were final losers the following season, this time to Dundee, who had earlier beaten Kilmarnock 1-0 in front of the lowest semi-final gate Hampden had ever seen – just 4,682. The next season, Celtic beat Hibs 6-3 to regain the trophy in a match that saw both sides score hat-tricks – Dixie Deans for Celts and Joe Harper for Hibs, the only man to score a hat-trick in a Hampden final and finish on the losing side.

Rangers won the 1975-76 final with a 1-0 win over their Old Firm rivals, and Celts also lost the next season's showdown as Aberdeen, under Ally MacLeod, won a thrilling match played in pouring rain thanks to a Davie Robb goal in extra time. Rangers snatched back the prize in the next campaign as Davie Cooper's first Hampden goal helped hand Celtic yet another final defeat. Gers retained the trophy in 1978-79, beating Aberdeen 2-1.

But the competition was in decline, with the Scottish League making constant changes in format and dates. The 1979-80 final attracted only 27,299, who watched a goal-less draw between Dundee United and Aberdeen. The ultimate insult came when the replay was moved from Hampden to Dens Park, Dundee, where a similar-sized crowd produced a full house and a better atmosphere as the Tangerines won their first national trophy.

★ ★ ★ ★ ★

AMID the usual round of home internationals and tournament qualifiers, Peru made the long journey to Hampden in 1972 only to be beaten 2-0 in front of just over 20,000 fans. There were almost 100,000 more inside the ground a month later when an Alan Ball goal gave England victory. Less than a year later, the SFA invited their oldest rivals England and World champions Brazil to Hampden to celebrate the association's centenary. Willie Ormond took charge of the Scots against England on February 14th, 1973, and he and the sparse crowd watched in stunned disbelief as his side was taken apart 5-0 in Hampden's own version of the St Valentine's Day Massacre.

It was a much-improved performance in June against Brazil, now minus Pele but containing the likes of Clodoaldo, Rivelino, Jairzinho and Dirceu. The new stars beat their hosts 1-0. The centenary defeats were hardly the best preparation for one of Scotland's most crucial games in their history.

Victory over Czechoslovakia would book Scotland's place in the 1974 World Cup Finals in West Germany. But after such a poor run of form and with a new manager yet to record a win, September 26th, 1973, was a nervous

GERMANY HERE WE COME: Captain Billy Bremner is held aloft as the Scotland team receive the cheers of the Hampden crowd after beating Czechoslovakia 2-1 to qualify for the 1974 World Cup Finals.

ON THE MARCH WITH ALLY'S ARMY:: Scotland's World Cup squad of 1978, led by Ally MacLeod, far left, is given a rousing send-off by 25,000 fans at Hampden before flying out to Argentina. Weeks later, they came home in shame after losing to Peru, drawing with Iran and having Willie Johnston banned for failing a drugs test.

night for the 95,786 fans who yelled non-stop encouragement at Hampden and for the hundreds of thousands in front of their TVs.

The lion-hearted Bremner skippered his team with trademark aggression as Scotland sought to break down the seven-man wall strung across the Czech defence. Law, Dalglish and Willie Morgan all had chances. Then disaster struck. Zdenek Nehoda fired in a shot that squirmed under Celtic keeper Ally Hunter and into the net. The nightmare of yet another World Cup failure stared Scotland in the face. But five minutes before the break, Jim Holton headed home a Law corner. The ground erupted: "Six foot two, eyes of blue, Big Jim Holton's after you."

In the second half, Ormond made a crucial change, sacrificing the artistry of Dalglish for the more direct approach of substitute Joe Jordan. In the 75th minute, Bremner let fly but the ball hit the inside of the post and bounced along the line and out of harm's way. Or so it seemed – but Morgan turned the ball back across goal for the inrushing Jordan to dive and head gloriously into the net.

This time the crowd let rip with a full-blooded Hampden Roar to match any heard in all the ground's illustrious past. After 16 painful years, Scotland were back in the World Cup Finals. Not a soul left the stadium until the team took the plaudits and the players raised Ormond shoulder high to take the acclaim of the fans.

It had been a night of raw emotion in which the low, intimidating growls of the hordes massed on the old stadium's darkened terraces had done much to sow the seeds of victory. That passion carried Scotland all the way to the finals and although they failed to reach the second stage on the flimsiest of goal differences, they came home as the tournament's only unbeaten team.

In a purple patch for the national team, they lost just once in 20 games over four years. Unfortunately, the defeat was against Spain in a European Championship match that ended the Scots' hope of reaching the 1976 finals – which were won by Czechoslovakia. The run also brought two welcome and overdue victories over England – including, in 1976, Dalglish's cheeky winner, hit between the legs of hapless Ray Clemence, that avenged all those Sassenach jibes about Scottish keepers.

The Czechs returned to Hampden in September 1977 as European champions but lost 3-1 as Scotland moved towards booking their place at the 1978 World Cup finals. An unlucky 1-0 home defeat against England was passed off as nothing more than a warm-up exercise for the action in Argentina.

The disappointment of the 1978 World Cup is best forgotten, as is the embarrassment of the pre-finals farewell ceremony at Hampden. But the Tartan Army displayed their legendary resolve by turning up in huge numbers for the

THE ULTIMATE NUTMEG: Hampden was the scene of England keeper Ray Clemence's most embarrassing moment as he let a Kenny Dalglish shot squirm through his legs for the winning goal in Scotland's 2-1 win over the Auld Enemy in 1976.

A GENIUS ARRIVES: The visit of world champions Argentina to Hampden in 1979 gave Scottish fans their first glimpse of the teenage sensation Diego Maradona... soon to be acknowledged as the best player on the planet. Although he is stopped here by a tackle from Scotland defender Paul Hegarty, he went on to score a wonder goal in a 3-1 win for the South Americans.

next home match – a European Championship qualifier against Norway that Scotland won 3-2. Despite the win, the Scots lost out in their group to a fine Belgian team that went on to reach the final in Rome.

There was little time for friendlies in the increasingly-congested fixture calendar but Scotland found room for two intriguing encounters in 1979. First came world champions Argentina, with their big names Passarella and Luque. But the real fascination was over an 18-year old forward who hadn't even been part of their 1978 squad. It was Scotland's chance to run the rule over Diego Armando Maradona, football's new phenomenon, tipped as the successor to Pele. More than 60,000 Scots left Hampden that evening, knowing they had been in the presence of true football greatness as the youngster capped a fine performance with a goal in Argentina's 3-1 win. Then Scotland drew 1-1 with Peru, the team that had beaten them in Argentina. A hectic 1980 itinerary began with a 4-1 victory over Portugal that concluded another fruitless European Championship campaign.

IT wasn't just big domestic games and internationals that sought the Hampden stage. Once again Celtic took a European Cup game across the city as they attempted to retrieve a three-goal deficit against Ajax Amsterdam in

DUTCH DEFIANCE: Ajax keeper Heinz Stuy punches the ball away from Celtic striker Harry Hood in the 1971 European Cup quarter-final. The Parkhead club switched three of their European ties to Hampden during the Seventies.

THREE IN A ROW: The Bayern Munich players show the European Cup off to the crowd at Hampden after their 1-0 win over French champions St Etienne in 1976. The result gave the Germans a hat-trick of victories following their wins in 1974 and 1975.

JUNIOR GIANTS: Cambuslang Rangers, in blue, on the attack against Bonnyrigg Rose in the 1972 Scottish Junior Cup Final which they won 3-2 in the replay after a 1-1 draw. The Lanarkshire side won three finals between 1971 and 1974, although they lost to Irvine Meadow in 1973 after two drawn matches at Hampden.

the 1971 quarter-finals. Over 83,000 saw the team of Krol, Keizer, Neeskens and the brilliant Johan Cruyff in action. Jimmy Johnstone's goal gave Celtic victory on the night but it was not enough to topple a team about to embark on a streak of three successive European Cup triumphs.

Due to building work at their own stadium, Celtic were back at Hampden again in 1972 to beat Norwegians Rosenborg, but the next big European night was reserved for the successors to Ajax as kings of the continent. After a gap of 16 years, the European Cup Final returned to Glasgow in 1976 with the French Champions St Etienne facing the winners for the past two seasons, Bayern Munich.

Star-studded Bayern oozed class from Sepp Maier in goal through Uli Hoeness on the wing to the lethal pairing of Karl-Heinz Rummenigge and Gerd Muller. They were led by the legendary Franz Beckenbauer. Yet it was one of Bayern's lesser-known players, Franz Roth, whose goal gave the Germans their third successive victory.

At a more modest, if equally intense level, Cambuslang Rangers were chasing their own treble after Junior Cup victories in 1967 and 1972. Their path to a third in 1973 was barred by Irvine Meadow. The evenly-matched sides were deadlocked after the final and a replay. The third tie, watched by almost 25,000 fans, saw an O'Brien penalty sealing the win for Meadow. Cambuslang were back in 1974 for a fourth successive final and this time they made no mistake, beating Linlithgow Rose 3-1 to set the seal on a remarkable era for the Junior game.

★ ★ ★ ★ ★

THE Ibrox Disaster cast a long shadow over Scottish football in the 1970s but eventually a series of licensing requirements forced the authorities to put crowd safety at the head of its priorities. Pittodrie and Ibrox were turned

SHAME GAME: The disgraceful scenes after the 1980 Scottish Cup Final at Hampden when fans invaded the pitch. The incident led to alcohol being banned from football grounds and to fences being erected at Hampden

....

into all-seater stadiums while capacities were slashed throughout the country.

Hampden's limit dropped 50,000 in the decade and plans were put forward to develop the ground into a modern stadium fit for the future.

But just as it appeared progress was being made, Scottish football was plunged into crisis. The 1980 Scottish Cup Final was another Old Firm affair won 1-0 by Celtic in extra time.

The result was immaterial. The final whistle signalled scenes reminiscent of the 1909 riot as supporters of both sides stormed the pitch and fought a running battle.

Mounted police made several cavalry charges before order was restored.

The supposed showpiece game of the domestic season ended in chaos

The game in Scotland was in a full-blown crisis. Something had to be done.

PARKING PROBLEM: Potholes cover the surface of the car park in this photograph of Hampden taken in the 1980s. Soon redevelopment work would take place.

HEART-BREAKER: John Hewitt celebrates after scoring for Aberdeen in their 3-0 Scottish Cup Final victory over Hearts in 1986. By this time, the terracings had been concreted, the North Stand knocked down and other improvements made. But there was still no cover – or seats – for the East or North Terracing.

Chapter 8

New Firm takes over at Fortress Hampden

THE authorities weren't long in taking action in the wake of the 1980 cup final riot. One of the great staples of generations of supporters – the "cairry oot" – vanished from the scene as a ban on drinking alcohol inside football grounds came into effect. Even cans and bottles of soft drink were banned, as they were now classed as potential "missiles". Local youths saw the end of their long-established cottage industry of lugging heavy bags full of clinking, clanking empty "ginger" bottles to nearby shops to claim the deposit of a few pence on each one.

Stewarding, too, came under greater scrutiny as professional security agencies replaced volunteer supporters. Scottish football began the climb back to respectability, with Hampden at the forefront. But it wasn't an easy route. Scotland was spared the horrors of the 1980s witnessed at Heysel, Bradford and Hillsborough, but bringing the National Stadium into the modern era was a journey with many perils along the way.

As well as the obvious problems of drunkenness, violence and sectarianism, football now faced hostility from a more dangerous quarter. Central government had traditionally distanced itself from the game – happy to lap up any plaudits and be in attendance when the medals were being handed out but careful to avoid direct involvement. In the 1980s, government was positively hostile to the game. Schemes to force fans to carry ID cards were hatched and given serious consideration. Ministerial allies inside the sport even mooted such outlandish and bizarre concepts as electric fences for penning fans.

With attendances dropping sharply, it wasn't a good time to be a football fan. The old ball game needed a shot in the arm and got it with a vibrant challenge to the Old Firm from Aberdeen, under Alex Ferguson and Dundee United, led by Jim McLean.

McLean's team had made the breakthrough by winning the League Cup twice, although both victories had been

WHAT A LOAD OF RUBBISH: The terraces are still littered after a big match in the 1970s but a game goes on with under 1,000 supporters.

170

at Dens Park, not Hampden. The National Stadium seemed to be something of a jinx for the Tannadice side as they reached – and lost – finals there on a regular basis.

The League Cup went to Celtic in 1982-83, to the delight of their joyous supporters, who seemed oblivious to the freezing rain which cascaded upon them on the roofless East Terracing as goals from Charlie Nicholas and Murdo MacLeod set up a 2-1 win over Rangers. Their great rivals gained revenge by beating the Bhoys 3-2 the following season with a hat-trick from Ally McCoist.

In 1985-86, Aberdeen beat Hibs 3-0, giving Alex Ferguson the one domestic trophy missing from his CV. Ironically, after Ferguson departed for Old Trafford and Graeme Souness arrived as manager at Ibrox, the Rangers-Aberdeen rivalry reached its peak. In the League Cup, the teams contested three successive close and exciting finals.

The epic 1987-88 contest ended after 120 minutes with the teams level at 3-3. The first major trophy in Scotland to be decided on penalty kicks went to Rangers, who held their nerve better than the Dons to win the shoot-out 5-3. An equally thrilling game took place 12 months later as Gers – aided by a McCoist double – squeezed home 3-2. But it was third time lucky for the Dons in 1989-90 when the match again went to extra-time before Aberdeen emerged victorious 2-1.

Rangers returned to see off Celtic the next season but 1991-92 showed that "outsiders" could still lift silverware as Hibernian beat Dunfermline 2-0. The familiar faces of Rangers and Aberdeen returned the following year and again it took extra time to separate them. Rangers emerged with the trophy, winning 2-1.

★ ★ ★ ★ ★

RANGERS held off Dundee United to win the Scottish Cup in a replayed final in 1981 and it seemed business as usual for the Old Firm – but that was the last the old trophy would be on display at Ibrox for over a decade. The Glaswegian grip on the cup wasn't so much broken as shattered into a thousand pieces by Ferguson and his Aberdeen team.

The manager instilled self-belief in his talented group of players and bred incredible loyalty, fostering a "we'll show them" mentality. The Pittodrie men looked a bit stage-struck at first against Rangers in the 1982 final, but after going behind they demolished Gers in extra-time to win 4-1. It's a tribute to the influence Ferguson wielded that all four

HAPPY HIBEES: The Hibernian squad show off the League Cup after their 2-0 win over Dunfermline in 1991.

scorers that day – Alex McLeish, Mark McGhee, Gordon Strachan and Neale Cooper – have followed him into management.

Just 10 days after lifting the European Cup-Winners' Cup in Gothenburg, Aberdeen were at Hampden to face Rangers in the 1983 showdown. Eric Black's header after 116 minutes settled the game. Immediately after the final whistle, Ferguson lambasted his players' performances live on TV in an incredible display, highlighting the standards he expected, even in beating the Old Firm in a Hampden cup final.

Celtic faced the Dons in the 1984 crunch clash. It was a bad-tempered affair. Black gave Aberdeen the lead but they failed to capitalise on their advantage even when Celtic were reduced to 10 men when captain Roy Aitken was sent off before the interval – the first player to be sent off in the final since 1929.

Paul McStay equalised with five minutes remaining to send the tie into extra-time for the third year running. By now the Dons took such events in their stride and McGhee's early goal capped a remarkable occasion, as

A TON OF FUN: Celtic captain Roy Aitken and matchwinner Frank McGarvey show the trophy to their fans at Hampden after winning the 100th Scottish Cup Final in 1985

Aberdeen won a third successive cup and also became the first team apart from the Old Firm to win a League and cup Double.

The Centenary Final may well have been in 1973, but due to wartime cancellations the actual 100th Final was played in 1985 when Celtic beat Dundee United 2-1 thanks to a free-kick from Davie Provan and a diving header from Frank McGarvey – who was sold to St Mirren weeks later.

The 1986 and 1987 Scottish Cups were remarkable as neither Old Firm club progressed as far as the semi-finals in either season.

In 1986, Aberdeen returned to take the trophy for the fourth time in five seasons with an easy 3-0 win over a dejected Hearts team that just seven days earlier had been on the brink of the League and Cup double. The Tynecastle team threw away the title to Celtic in the dying minutes of their last league game at Dundee and never recovered in time to mount a challenge at Hampden. Dundee United also had a double in their sights in 1987. Their two-legged UEFA Cup final straddled the Scottish Cup Final and the distraction may have helped opponents St Mirren. After a goal-less 90 minutes, Saints clinched the trophy for the first time in 28 years when Ian Ferguson netted late in extra-time.

Hampden resounded to a new beat the following month when it hosted its first pop concert. Ian Anderson of

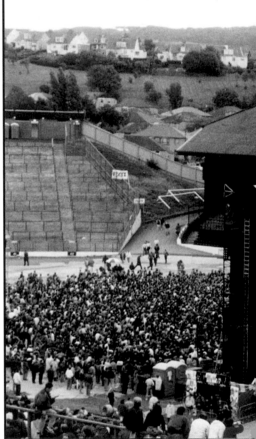

HONKY TONK HAMPDEN: The Rolling Stones hired the National Stadium in 1990 to host the Scottish leg of their Urban Jungle Tour. The front of the South Stand was transformed into a huge stage, right, and the props included a massive inflatable woman. The tiny figure at the bottom of the picture on the left is Stones singer Mick Jagger!

Jethro Tull had refused a £10,000 offer to appear there as far back as 1970 but Paul Young headlined a concert that proved a huge hit with 30,000 fans. Three years on and the Rolling Stones' Urban Jungle Tour hit the road and pitched its tent at Hampden on 9th July to give Queen's Park a special 123rd birthday party.

Back to the more mundane, if more traditional gig, and Dundee United played Hampden yet again in 1988 and lost to Celtic again. A late double from Frank McAvennie gave Celtic the perfect present for their club centenary – a league and cup double. The Hoops retained the trophy in 1989, a Joe Miller goal pipping Rangers 1-0, to set up a crack at a third successive Scottish Cup. Celts were favourites to beat Aberdeen but after 90 minutes and extra-time, the teams were locked at 0-0. For the first time, the Scottish Cup would be won and lost on penalty kicks.

Both sides missed once from the initial five kicks but kept pace with each other after that. The shoot-out score

BLACK AND WHITE DELIGHT: St Mirren manager Alex Smith, right, is raised shoulder high by players Kenny McDowall and Neil Cooper as he celebrates the Paisley side's Scottish Cup triumph in 1987. Alex also won the cup in 1990 as manager of Aberdeen.

was 8-8 when Celtic's Anton Rogan stepped up to the mark and recoiled in horror as keeper Theo Snelders saved. The spotlight was on Brian Irvine, only in the Aberdeen team as a replacement for the injured Willie Miller. Irvine kept his nerve and the 20th penalty was despatched past Pat Bonner to win the trophy for Aberdeen 9-8 on penalties.

Success was especially sweet for Dons boss Alex Smith who had been in charge of St Mirren three years previously. Winning with the Dons made him the first manager since Jock Stein to win the cup at two clubs.

Dramatic as it was, the 1990 showdown lacked goals – a charge impossible to level at the next final. That old cliché "the family final" really did apply to the meeting of Motherwell and Dundee United, as Tommy McLean led the Lanarkshire side to their first final in 39 years while brother Jim bossed United to their sixth under his command.

More than 57,000 fans converged on Hampden and were served up a feast of football. Ian Ferguson opened for Well in 32 minutes but the Steelmen suffered a blow when keeper Ally Maxwell suffered a rib injury. He had to play on, but United took advantage. Dave Bowman equalised before Phil O'Donnell restored Well's lead. Then Ian Angus made it 3-1 before Michael O'Neill's header kept United in the hunt. With 60 seconds left, Darren

THE FAMILY FINAL: The McLean brothers Jim, left, and Tommy lead out their Dundee United and Motherwell sides for the 1991 Scottish Cup Final at Hampden.

Jackson equalised for the Taysiders and again a final went to extra-time.

Four minutes into the first period, Steve Kirk crashed home a fourth goal for Well and this time exhausted United had no reply. For the sixth time in 17 years they stood and watched as their opponents lifted the trophy.

Airdrie attempted to make it a Lanarkshire double in 1992 but Rangers were just that bit better. It had been 11 years since the Ibrox side last tasted Scottish Cup glory and it was the one trophy that eluded Souness in his five-year reign as manager. His successor, Walter Smith, won at the first time of asking as goals from Mark Hateley and Ally McCoist ended their Scottish Cup drought.

★ ★ ★ ★ ★

FORTRESS Hampden is an apt description of the National Stadium in the 1980s. Between December 1979 and April 1990, no continental European country won at the stadium. The handful of defeats suffered by the Scots at home were dished out by traditional rivals England, Wales and the Republic of Ireland, in addition to one by Brazil. It was a remarkable record and the envy of any nation.

That near-invincibility at home helped carry Scotland, now managed by Jock Stein, to the World Cup in Spain in 1982 when, for the third time in succession, goal difference prevented them from progressing to the second stage.

Unfortunately, performances away from Hampden did not nearly match the home record and Scotland failed to qualify for the 1984 European Championship. The same year, and after exactly 100 years, the Home Internationals were discontinued, chiefly at the behest of Scotland and England who claimed the fixture calendar was too congested. The series ended with a 1-1 draw with England and a slap in the face from Northern Ireland and Wales who finished first and

ACCLAIM AND APATHY: Scotland captain Graeme Souness, above, is cheered by the Hampden crowd as he hoists the Rous Cup in 1985 after a 1-0 win over England. Four years later, the terraces are all but empty, right, as Peter Grant moves in to make a tackle in Scotland's match against Chile in the same tournament.

second in the table – with Scotland bottom. The Scots geared up for the 1986 World Cup qualifiers with a memorable 6-1 demolition of a strong Yugoslavia side with six different players sharing the goals.

The campaign started with a victory over Iceland before Scotland beat European Championships runners-up Spain 3-1 – with Kenny Dalglish memorably spinning and thundering the ball into the roof of the net for the second goal.

But the Welsh threw qualification back into the melting pot with a 1-0 win at Hampden and it took a plucky and lucky draw in Cardiff to keep the Mexico dream alive. Tragically, Stein collapsed and died that night as his team struggled through to the World Cup play-offs.

Stein's last game in charge at Hampden had been the Rous Cup, invented to replace the old Home Internationals. Richard Gough's beautifully-headed goal in May 1985 was enough for a satisfactory defeat of England.

It is difficult to overstate the place of Stein in the pantheon of Scottish greats. He was the man who brought the European Cup to Scotland and restored respect to the national side during a low point in their history. As Bill Shankly told him on that glorious night in Lisbon, Stein is "an immortal".

Stein's baton was picked up on a temporary basis by Alex Ferguson. The Aberdeen boss combined his club job with managing Scotland for the duration of the World Cup campaign. He led Scotland to victory over Australia and a place in the finals in Mexico. But even Fergie's drive could not improve Scotland's dismal record as again they failed to get past the first round. Another Queen's Park old boy, Andy Roxburgh, took over as Scotland boss but could do nothing to improve the team's European Championship record.

The Rous Cup was expanded to include South American teams, and Brazil were popular visitors in 1987 – but the experiment was not a success. The competition was wound up – and with it the 117-year old series against England in 1989. It was a timid farewell as Scotland lost 2-0 to England then beat Chile by the same score in front of just 9,006 fans – the second lowest international gate at Hampden.

When it really mattered, Hampden could still pack 'em in and 65,204 manned the classic slopes in March 1989 for a World Cup qualifying match against France. The French were one of the best teams in the world and had a pretty impressive pedigree, having won the European Championship in 1984 and reached a couple of World Cup semi-finals. The man of the match plied his trade in the French League – but wore the dark blue of Scotland. Maurice Johnston, then with Nantes, was at the peak of his powers and his goals – one in each half – that took Scotland to the brink of their fifth successive qualification.

Scotland needed just one point from their last three games to book a plane to Italy for Euro '90. True to form they waited to the very last to clinch their place, losing in Yugoslavia and France before drawing 1-1 with Norway at Hampden.

The warm-up programme for Italy included a visit from world champions Argentina. There was no Maradona but it was still a stiff test – and one that the home side passed with flying colours with Stewart McKimmie scoring the only goal. After that came defeat by East Germany in the last international

HANDS UP IF YOU'RE ABOUT TO LOSE A GOAL: Maurice Johnston has the French pleading in vain for offside as he scores for Scotland in a vital World Cup qualifying match at Hampden in 1989.

WORLD BEATER: Stewart McKimmie celebrates scoring the winner against Argentina in 1989. The Aberdeen full-back was the unlikely goal hero as Scotland beat the reigning World Cup holders 1-0 at Hampden.

VINTAGE PERFORMANCE: Junior Cup winners Pollok make an unusual lap of honour at Hampden in 1981.

match played by the GDR before German reunification. It was "as you were" for the finals in Italy as Scotland again flew home at the end of the first stage.

Just 12,801 made the effort to attend the European Championship qualifier against Romania despite the presence of the "Maradona of the Carpathians" Gheorghe Hagi. Goals from John Robertson and Ally McCoist gave the Scots a fighting win and at last they mounted a serious bid at European level. In a tough group with Switzerland and Bulgaria as well as Romania and makeweights San Marino, Scotland just squeezed through.

After seven attempts the Scots had finally qualified for the finals of the European Championships. Their performances in Gothenburg and Norrkoping deserved better than the traditional homeward journey at the end of the first round.

★ ★ ★ ★ ★

IN 1986, the SJFA celebrated its centenary and there could have been no other venue for the 100th Junior Cup

PAY AND ENTER: Over the decades millions of fans passed through these old turnstiles to watch the best footballers of the day.

Final than Hampden Park. Two of the biggest names contested the final – Pollok, from Glasgow, were the holders and Auchinleck Talbot, from Ayrshire, had won six of the last seven West of Scotland Cups.

A strike double from Tom MacDonald and a goal by Jim O'Donnell gave Talbot a historic win in a hard-fought clash that had seen Pollok go 2-0 up before the Ayrshire men mounted their fightback. It was the start of a golden age for Auchinleck – but it had nothing to do with the National Stadium ... Hampden Park had held its last Junior Cup Final.

SCOTLAND hosted FIFA's 1989 Under-16 World Cup Finals and the Scots did extremely well to reach the Hampden final where they had the misfortune to face a distinctly "mature" Saudi Arabian side and lost 5-4 on penalties having drawn 2-2 after extra time.

In a tournament that introduced Scots to the talents of Luis Figo, Claudio Reyna and Serginho, it was an excellent achievement for Scotland's James Will who became the first keeper to win the "Golden Ball" as Player of the Tournament. And, of course, more than 50,000 Scots in attendance could claim to have seen Scotland play in a World Cup Final at Hampden Park!

YOUTH TAKES A BOW: Scotland captain Brian O'Neil evades the challenge of a Saudi Arabian player during the FIFA World Under-16 Championships Final at Hampden Park in 1989. O'Neil, who went on to be capped for the full Scotland side, missed a spot kick during the match, which the Scots eventually lost on penalties.

LEGENDS REUNITED: Former Scotland boss Tommy Docherty joins Alex Ferguson in a salute to the legendary Kenny Dalglish as the 102-times capped striker takes a bow during his testimonial match at Hampden in 1986. Fergie managed a team of home-based Scots who lost to the Doc's Anglo select. Dalglish played for both teams.

WORK BEGINS: The redevelopment of the open terracing at Hampden begins in 1993. It was the start of the project which led to the magnificent stadium we see today.

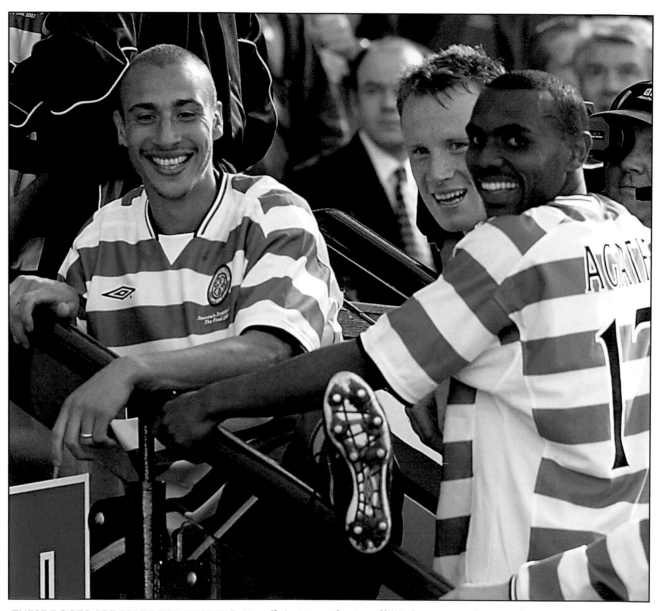

THESE BOOTS ARE MADE FOR SCORING: Henrik Larsson shows off his footwear after scoring twice against Hibs in the 2001 Scottish Cup Final. Earlier that year he hit a hat-trick in the League Cup Final against Kilmarnock

Chapter 9

The Glory Returns to the World's Finest Stadium

ALL the facelifts, building work and reconstruction couldn't hide the simple truth. Hampden Park was nearly 90 and looked its age. The fans said farewell to the "classic slopes" at the League Cup Final in October 1992. After Rangers' victory over Aberdeen, the bulldozers moved in.

It marked the first phase in the grand conversion to turn Hampden into a stadium fit for a new century. The huge ash covered terraces were a thing of the past.

The ground more or less slipped out of commission for major matches, hosting just one of the next six League Cup Finals – Aberdeen's 2-0 win over Dundee in November 1995. The League Cup returned in March 2000 to a stadium that might have had the same name but was almost unrecognisable – and Celtic won the first prize of the new millennium with a 2-0 win over Aberdeen.

A year later, a virtuoso performance from Swedish striker Henrik Larsson retained the trophy for 10-man Celtic after Chris Sutton was sent off against Kilmarnock. Even without his striking partner, Larsson still notched up the first Hampden hat-trick of the 21st century in Celtic's 3-0 triumph.

There was another Glasgow-Ayrshire contest in season 2001-2002 as Ayr United reached the first major final in their 92-year history. They enjoyed their big day and Rangers enjoyed a big win – 4-0 – with Argentinian legend Claudo Caniggia bagging two goals.

New Rangers boss Alex McLeish greeted his first trophy triumph by criticising his players' first-half performance. His mentor Ferguson would have approved.

No such outbursts from McLeish in 2003, as his side beat Celtic in a thriller. Caniggia and Peter Lovenkrands

AYR RAIDERS: Fans outside Hampden before their Scottish League Cup Final against Rangers in 2002.

gave Gers a 2-0 half-time lead but Larsson's header in 56 minutes brought Celtic back into the game. Six minutes later, a John Hartson strike was ruled offside – although TV evidence indicated it was the wrong decision – then the Wales striker missed a last-minute penalty as Rangers held on to win 2-1 and clinch the first leg of the domestic treble.

★ ★ ★ ★ ★

THE Scottish Cup briefly decamped to Ibrox but by April 1994 the partially-rebuilt Hampden was ready for business. Inside 11 months, the new east and west stands had been constructed and some of the facts and figures used to illustrate the scale of the task are stupendous.

It had taken the equivalent amount of steel for 4,500 average family cars, enough bricks to build over 20 three-bed semi-detached houses, electrical cabling that would have stretched from Glasgow to Penrith and almost 36 years of labour. And of course, this was only phase two. It still wasn't finished, but with a capacity of 38,000, the ground could host big games again.

The new pitch was rigorously tested with two semi-finals and their replays in five April days, with Dundee

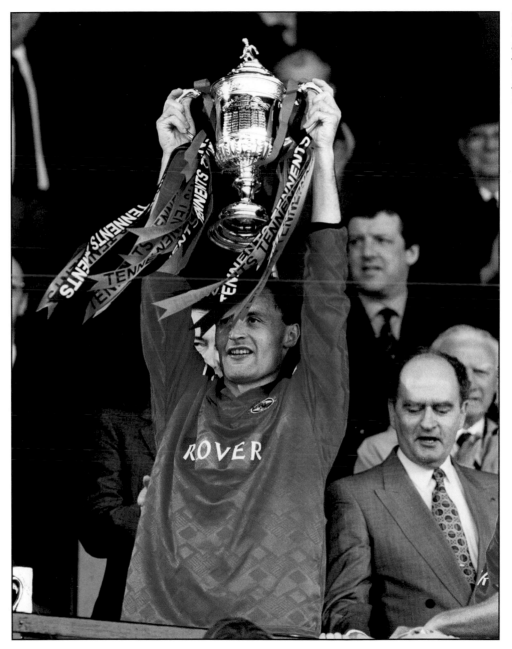

UNITED WE STAND:
Hampden witnesses
another Scottish Cup
triumph as Maurice
Malpas lifts the trophy
for Dundee United in
1994.

TAKING SHAPE: The South Stand is still being demolished and only two sides of the ground are complete. Temporary changing facilities have been provided for Queen's Park games.

HE WEARS IT WELL: Rocker Rod Stewart is a regular visitor to Hampden. He was in the crowd, above, to watch Celtic win the Scottish Cup in 1995 when they beat Airdrie and met with another legend – Lisbon Lion Jimmy Johnstone, left. Comedian Tony Roper is also in the crowd, above.

United and Rangers emerging to take their places in the final. United's Ivan Golac was the first foreign manager of a Scottish club and had his own style of management.

The decisive moment was early in the second half when a blunder by Gers keeper Ally Maxwell let in United's Christian Dailly, whose shot ran along the line and back off a post, giving team-mate Craig Brewster a simple close-range tap-in. At their seventh attempt, spanning two decades, Dundee United had at last got their hands on the Scottish Cup.

Six years without a trophy is an eternity for Old Firm fans, so Celtic's 1995 victory was sweet. Pierre Van Hooijdonk's early goal ended Airdrie's hopes and no-one was happier than manager Tommy Burns – it was the only silver moment in his spell in the Parkhead hotseat.

The 1996 final was the most one-sided since 1972 and again a Glasgow team demolished Edinburgh opposition. This time the winners were Rangers and the losers – nay, victims – Hearts. Walter Smith's team strolled to a 5-1 victory with a hat-trick for Gordon Durie and a double from the superb Brian Laudrup.

It was time for the Scottish Cup to take another break from Hampden as the stadium embarked on the final stage of reconstruction and both Kilmarnock and Hearts celebrated their 1997 and 1998 wins elsewhere.

It was also time for Hampden's most famous landmark to take its final bow. The South Stand succumbed to the demolisher's ball and chain in November 1997. Perhaps the chill wind caused the tears in the eyes of the onlookers. However, perhaps they were recalling the hundreds of brave fightbacks for famous wins, the heartache of a last-minute defeat, the echo of the Roar, the cups eagerly brandished to ecstatic fans, cheering on the promotion sides, "Remember when..."

The old order was in place when Hampden

OUCH: Aberdeen keeper Jim Leighton is injured in a clash with Rod Wallace of Rangers in the 2000 Cup Final

reported back for duty in its magnificent, shiny new suit. Rangers carved out a victory over Celtic in 1999 courtesy of a Rod Wallace goal and retained the trophy with an easy 4-0 win over Aberdeen the next season.

The game brought down the curtain on the career of Jim Leighton in the cruellest of fashions. The game had run scarcely two minutes when the keeper plunged at the feet of an attacker, leaving him bloody and dazed. The Dons had no substitute keeper, so forward Robbie Winters took Leighton's place.

In his first season as manager, Martin O'Neill took Celtic to Hampden in 2001 where only Hibs – whose last cup win had been 99 years previously – stood between the club and their first treble since 1969. Larsson was in the form of his life and his two goals, plus one from Jackie McNamara, made it a day to remember for the Bhoys.

The Old Firm were back for the 2002 final and they served up one of the best finals of recent years. Twice Celtic took the lead through Hartson and Bobo Balde but Gers levelled through Lovenkrands and Barry Ferguson. With just seven seconds left, Lovenkrands smashed home the winner in a spectacular finale.

Rangers returned to Hampden on the last day of May 2003 to face Dundee, who quickly made a mockery of predictions of an easy Ibrox triumph. Barry Smith rattled a post after four minutes and the Dark Blues had the hallmark of winners. The pair were still deadlocked midway through the second half when Lorenzo Amoruso timed his run to perfection and bulleted a header past Dundee keeper Julian Speroni for the game's only goal. It

THE BOSS MEN: Alex McLeish, of Rangers and Dundee's Jim Duffy show the strain during the 2003 Scottish Cup Final

was to be the big Italian's last game for Rangers and he cried a river of tears as he toured the stadium with the famous trophy.

★ ★ ★ ★ ★

HAMPDEN played no part in the dismal 1994 World Cup qualifying campaign – Scotland's first failure for almost a quarter of a century. Holland visited in March 1994 for a friendly to mark the reopening of the ground but spoiled the party with a 1-0 win – the only reverse for the Scots in 15 games at Hampden between April 1990 and November 1999.

Four home wins and a draw helped Scotland, now managed by Craig Brown, to Euro 96 in England. They drew

THE WORLD'S BEST: Hampden is now a magnificent stadium which is capable of hosting world class football matches, rock concerts or any other occasion where large crowds need to gather.

with Holland, lost to England and beat the Swiss, but lost out on goal difference, a now depressingly regular method of exiting major events for the Tartan Army.

Scotland returned to a nomadic existence, as games were taken round the country while the final stage of rebuilding Hampden was in progress. They reached the World Cup Finals in France in 1998 but again were home before the postcards.

They didn't return to Hampden until October 1999 after a gap of more than three and a half years.

The 3-0 win over Lithuania in their final qualifier was a welcome morale-booster for their next game – against England. After a 10-year absence, the Auld Enemy returned to Hampden for a play-off to determine which country would advance to the European Championship Finals in Belgium and Holland in 2000.

Over 50,000 assembled at Hampden and tested the recently-refurbished structure to its foundations with a wall of noise as the teams emerged at the start. But the game itself was a huge disappointment. A double from Paul Scholes left the Scots with an almost impossible task in the second leg at Wembley. They dominated the return match but Don Hutchison's headed goal was scant reward for their efforts.

Scotland still had something to celebrate in 2000. The rebuilt Hampden was officially opened with a match against world champions France. The

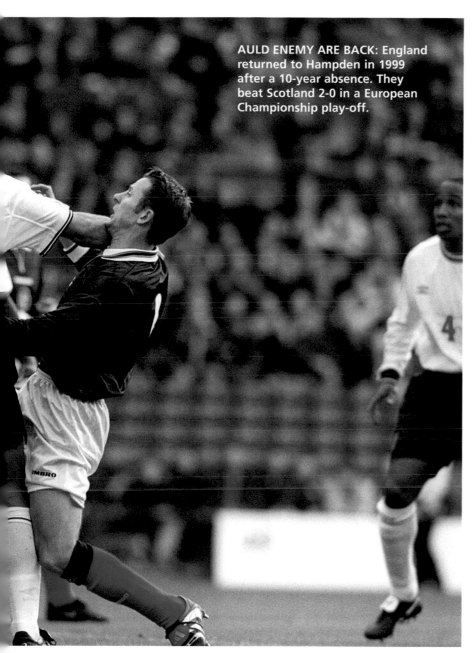

AULD ENEMY ARE BACK: England returned to Hampden in 1999 after a 10-year absence. They beat Scotland 2-0 in a European Championship play-off.

sublimely talented French attracted a near-full house and the reward was worth the 2-0 defeat – almost! Sylvain Wiltord put France ahead early in the second period and Thierry Henry added the second with a strike a minute from time.

Soon it was back to the nitty-gritty of World Cup qualification and Scotland bowled along merrily en route to the finals in the Far East until 60 minutes into a crucial Hampden game against Belgium. Two goals from Billy Dodds in the first half-hour had put the Scots in the driving seat, but the Belgians, by now down to 10 men, pulled a goal back and with the home fans whistling for time, Daniel Van Buyten powered in a header from 15 yards to square the game at 2-2.

The Scots beat San Marino easily enough but a listless 0-0 draw against Croatia and defeat in Belgium left them needing a huge win in their last tie against Latvia and a Belgian win over Croatia to make a play-off spot – but in the event got neither. Even the 2-1 win over Latvia was somewhat undeserved.

Despite all his meticulous planning and clever tactics, Craig Brown decided he could not take the side any further and, after nine years, he called it a day.

★ ★ ★ ★ ★

AFTER an absence of more than 90 years, Hampden welcomed back the oval ball game in 1999 when Scotland defeated Romania 60-19 in a warm-up game for that year's Rugby World Cup. Hampden also staged a one-sided group

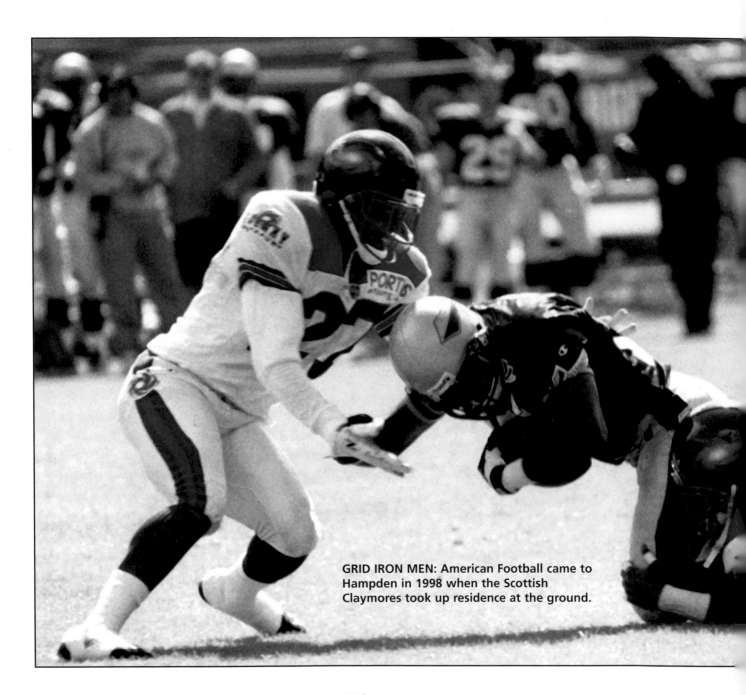

GRID IRON MEN: American Football came to Hampden in 1998 when the Scottish Claymores took up residence at the ground.

game between South Africa and Uruguay that saw the Springboks stroll to a 39-3 win.

The 1990s brought American Football in the shape of the Scottish Claymores – now the only British team in the NFL Europe. The Claymores had been around since 1995 and won the World Bowl in 1996 but first played at Hampden in 1998.

Appropriately, given that city's part in Hampden's most famous contest, their first opponents were Frankfurt Galaxy, who won a close encounter 15-12.

By 2001, Hampden had become the Claymores' exclusive home and they attracted a record 16,387 crowd for a narrow 24-21 win over Frankfurt. Testimony to the growing popularity of the sport came in June 2003 when the World Bowl came to Hampden and 28,138 fans turned up to watch two German teams do battle. The game was preceded by all the razzmatazz associated with the sport with a special Scottish flavouring added.

Music acts such as Mis-teeq, the Cosmic Rough Riders and Fish were accompanied by 100 pipers and the orchestra of the Royal Scottish Academy of Music and Drama, as well as the more familiar cheerleaders.

The Red Arrows put on a fly-past but the pre-match high point for those in the stadium and the 150 million households watching worldwide was the presence of the famous One o'clock Gun, whose daily boom is usually heard from the battlements of Edinburgh Castle.

On loan for the day, the cannon's roar started the action and, in an entertaining game, Frankfurt Galaxy scooping the prize with a 35-16 victory over Dusseldorf-based Rhein Fire. A Frankfurt win at Hampden? Forty-three years on, Eintracht must have been envious.

THE glitz of the World Bowl beds in well with Hampden's new-found status as a world events venue. Now, it's on the circuit for tours by the planet's biggest names. Rod Stewart, one-time Brentford trialist and adopted member of the Tartan Army rocked Hampden, wowing fans with his nifty footwork

IT'S A DIFFERENT BALL GAME: Hampden Park was selected to host American Football's prestigious World Bowl in 2003 and 28,138 fans turned up to watch Frankfurt Galaxy take on Rhein Fire.

RUN WITH THE BALL: Rugby returned to Hampden in 1999 when Scotland played Romania in a World Cup match (Page 203).

when he headlined the inaugural concert at the refurbished ground in July 1999. He also turned out for an All-Stars select which played Queen's Park in the first match at the revamped ground.

Tina Turner's 24/7 Millennium Tour rolled into town in 2000. The following summer, three of the biggest acts in the world visited the National Stadium. First there was Bon Jovi, whose One Wild Night tour lived up to its name. Next, thousands of Eagles fans lapped up the band's full repertoire, from Take It Easy to Hotel California. The long, hot summer was rounded off with two gigs from British singer Robbie Williams, whose plea to Let Me Entertain You was received enthusiastically by an adoring audience.

While their fathers and grandfathers may have had posters of Slim Jim on their walls, teens in the 21st century are more likely to be aficionados of Slim Shady. They got their chance to see their hero when rap star Eminem played Hampden in June 2003, with more than 40,000 snapping up tickets for his Anger Management Tour. The Health Education Board for Scotland (HEBS) sponsored a massive day-long festival entitled Live 'N' Loud in July 2003 with the aim of making a connection between music and health concerns. More than 30,000 young people were there to see current headliners such as Kym Marsh, Blue, Liberty X, Sugababes, Girls Aloud, Dannii Minogue, Busted, and Scotland's own David Sneddon and Darius.

★ ★ ★ ★ ★

BIG-TIME boxing returned to Hampden after an absence of over half a century when Mike Tyson took on Lou

LOUD 'N' PROUD: Hampden has rocked with the stars of the music world on many occasions with performers such as, from left – Tina Turner, and Darius Danesh, Rod Stewart, Kym Marsh and Robbie Williams

Savarese in a heavyweight bout on June 24th, 2000. It may have been Midsummer Night but it turned out more nightmare than dream. Around 20,000 fight fans welcomed Iron Mike into the ring at 11.50pm. Before midnight struck, they were making their way home.

Within 12 seconds of the first bell, Savarese was floored by a left hook. He rose shakily to be met with a flurry of hooks and uppercuts that forced the referee to stop the fight after just 38 seconds of the first round. But as he tried to separate the fighters, the referee himself was knocked to the canvas by Tyson, whose trainer had to leap into the ring to assure his fighter that the contest was over.

By coincidence, the bout was staged on the anniversary of the Battle of Bannockburn. While no one expected to see a punch-up of that quality, the crowd did at least expect a run for its money. Tyson, who had entered to the cheers of his fans, departed the ring to a chorus of boos .

★ ★ ★ ★ ★

SO Hampden Park has seen it all. From the cloth-capped crowds of the Edwardian era right through to the designer-clad youth of today. From the days of wooden ricketies to the organised dances of cheerleaders. From

BIG HITTER: Iron Mike Tyson punches his way to an easy win against Lou Savarese at Hampden in 2000. But many in the crowd weren't too happy with the fight and the outcome.

SAVE THE JERSEYS: The Hampden grass is covered with football strips donated as part of a charity campaign in June 2001.

flocks of pigeons carrying results all over Scotland to instant updates over the internet to the entire world. And the focal point of it all has been football: always football.

Because of today's needs, the crowds at Hampden may not be in the six-figure bracket, as they were in the first half of last century, but the ground has kept its soul and its place in the hearts of the Scottish people.

No one who was at Hampden to see Scotland face Germany in a qualifying match for the 2004 European Championship would have doubted that.

The voices of 48,047 Scotland fans rose in acclaim as their team took the field and not once did they let up during the 90 minutes that followed.

The doomsday merchants who had proclaimed the death of the Hampden Roar were forced to eat their words. A low rumble began to swell from within the stands, building to a full-throated crescendo as Scotland took the game to the Germans time and time again.

Even when Germany took the lead midway through the first half, the home team refused to buckle and, spurred on by the fans, continued to show they were the equal of a team that only 12 months before had played in the World Cup Final.

But time ran on and still the Germans led. Even the most diehard fan in the crowd began to wonder if there was any way back.

Then came a flash of ingenuity. Scotland won a free-kick and while the Germans ambled into position, Colin Cameron seized the moment and touched the ball forward to his Wolves·teammate Kenny Miller. Miller took one touch and stroked the ball past keeper Oliver Kahn and into the net.

Pandemonium! In the stands, pubs, clubs and living rooms around the globe, Scots howled their appreciation of a pride reborn.

The match finished 1-1 but from the reaction of the crowd anyone innocently switching on a television would have thought the World Cup itself was being paraded round Hampden.

The Hampden Roar dead? As Mark Twain would have said, reports of its demise are an exaggeration.

For 100 years Scotland and Hampden have been synonymous with each other. The national team and the National Stadium have a shared heritage, a past they can both look back on with pride.

Scotland will begin their second century at Hampden with a double century of their own. The 200th international match at Hampden lies in the near future.

It is a future that Scotland and Hampden will face together. One they need not fear.

A future filled with hope.

RETURN OF THE ROAR: The outlook is good for both the Scotland team and for Hampden Park – one of the world's greatest sporting venues.

PITCH PERFECT: The Hampden grass after the Tennents Scottish Cup Final between Rangers and Celtic in 2002. It is still in great shape, despite a pulsating game and the enthusiastic celebrations afterwards.

Hampden Milestones

1904 – 64,472 Scottish Cup Final Celtic v Rangers
First final at the Third Hampden Park

1906 – 102,741 Scotland v England
First six figure crowd in Scotland.

1908 – 121, 452 Scotland v England
World record gate for any game at the time.

1912 – 127,307 Scotland v England
World record gate for any game at the time.

1925 – 101,714 Scottish Cup Semi Final Celtic v Rangers
First six figure crowd for a club game in Scotland.

1928 – 118,115 Scottish Cup Final Rangers v Celtic
Record gate for a domestic match in Scotland

1930 – 95,772 Queen's Park FC v Rangers
World record gate for a competitive game involving an amateur league club.

1931 – 129,810 Scotland v England
World record gate for any game at the time.

1933 – 136,259 Scotland v England
World record gate for any game at the time.

1937 – 147,365 Scottish Cup Final Celtic v Aberdeen
All time world record gate for a national cup final.

1937 – 149,415 Scotland v England
All time world record gate for a European international.

1944 – 133,000 Scotland v England
Record wartime gate in Britain.

1945 – 133,000 Southern League Cup Final Rangers v Aberdeen
World record for a wartime club competition

1946 – 139, 468 Scotland v England
World record gate for an unofficial international.

1948 – 143,570 Scottish Cup Semi Final Rangers v Hibernian
World record gate for a non-national Final game.

1948 – 129,176 and 133,570 Scottish Cup Final and Replay Rangers v Greenock Morton
World record aggregate gate for a national final.

1954 – 113,056 Scotland v Hungary
All time record gate for a match involving Hungary.

**1960 – 127,621 European cup Final
Real Madrid v Eintracht Frankfurt**
All time record gate for a European Cup Final.

1963 – 105,907 League Cup Final Rangers v Morton
First six figure crowd for the League Cup.

1965 – 107,609 League Cup Final Celtic v Rangers
All time record gate for a British League Cup Final.

**1961 – 104,679 Floodlights commissioned
Rangers v Eintracht Frankfurt**
First six figure attendance for a non-competitive match

1964 – 133,245 Scotland v England
John White's last game at Hampden.

1970 – 136,505 Celtic v Leeds United
All time record for a European Cup game.